PENGUIN BOOKS

THE STILL POINT O

A former Fulbright scholar and gr   y
Rapp is the author of *Poster Child:*   e
New York Times, Salon, and *Slate,* am   t
of a Rona Jaffe Writers' Award, a
versity of Texas-Austin, and the F   g
fellowship at Bucknell University. She is a faculty member in the University
of California-Riverside MFA Program.

Praise for Emily Rapp's
The Still Point of the Turning World

"A brilliant study of the wages of mortal love."
—Sarah Manguso, *The New York Times Book Review*

"Rapp writes with . . . radiant honesty and intelligence, pulling you close,
making you care. She searches for solace in literature, religion, and friends,
joining forces with other 'dragon mothers' and finding the strength to protect and honor Ronan while preparing to let him go. . . . Rapp fights to
redefine the meaning of parenting—and of life itself. Living in the moment
is something we're told to aim for; she does it, finding profound joy in the
pure expression of love."   —Helen Rogan, *People* (4 star review)

"Emily Rapp's *The Still Point of the Turning World* . . . moves from shock to a
kind of stoic joy in her account of the brief life of her son, Ronan, who was
diagnosed with Tay-Sachs at nine months, a verdict that forced the author
to revise everything she imagined parenthood to be."

—Megan O'Grady, *Vogue*

"Rapp has an emotional accessibility reminiscent of *Wild* author Cheryl
Strayed; her unique experiences have a touch of the universal. She comes
across as open, midthought. In her book, she wrestles with the ideas of luck
and sentimentality and life and love and often circles back, unresolved.
Despite being a former divinity student, she bypasses religion for literature,
seeking meaning in poetry, myth, and, especially, *Frankenstein* and its author,
Mary Shelley. . . . Her kind of parent? The dragon mother: powerful, sometimes terrifying, full of fire and magic."

—Carolyn Kellogg, *Los Angeles Times*, ("Faces to Watch in 2013")

"An impassioned and searing account of loving—and preparing to lose—
her baby . . . A graduate of Harvard Divinity School, Rapp combines an
essayist's willingness to lay herself bare on the page, a theologian's search to
plumb the mysteries of life, and a poet's precision. The result is stunning. . . .

Although her subject is extremely sad, her book isn't depressing, because depression is a state of stasis, and Rapp actively investigates her grief, making something meaningful out of it."

—Malena Waltrous, *San Francisco Chronicle*

"A beautiful, searing exploration of the landscape of grief and a profound meditation on the meaning of life."   —*Kirkus Reviews* (starred review)

"Ronan's 'death sentence' was for Rapp and her husband, Rick, living in Santa Fe, a time of grief, reckoning, and learning how to live, and her elegant, restrained work flows with reflections and excerpts from writers and poets like Mary Shelley, Pablo Neruda, and Sylvia Plath, as well as supporters who helped her during the difficult unraveling of her son's condition. Writing about Ronan allowed her to claim the sorrow and truly look at her son the way he was. . . . Unflinching and unsentimental, Rapp's work lends a useful, compassionate, healing message for suffering parents and caregivers."

—*Publishers Weekly* (starred review)

"This memoir of extraordinary tenderness and grace in the face of unimaginable loss is searingly beautiful in the way of a sacred text. Emily Rapp certainly didn't sign on to be our guide into the deepest crevasses of the human heart, but that is what she has become. Of course this is an undeniably sad book, but don't let that stop you. It is also one of the most powerfully alive books I have ever read. Every page shouts: This is what it is to love! To risk! To lose! To bear witness! An unforgettable moral and artistic triumph."   —Dani Shapiro, author of *Devotion* and *Slow Motion*

"Although Rapp avoids sentimentality, her radiant book is steeped in deep feelings. . . . Readers nursing terminal patients of any age can find encouragement in Rapp's savored 'still point.' Her determination to envelop her son in love, protect him from as much suffering as possible, and then let him go is a protocol as applicable to an Alzheimer's patient as to a sick child."

—Heller McAlpin, *Los Angeles Times*

"Rapp is a deep and gifted storyteller. . . . [*The Still Point of the Turning World*] offers us the precise combination of vividness and distance necessary to think through the unthinkable."   —Katie Roiphe, *Slate*

"Rapp refuses to let this memoir be a woe-is-me discussion of the nightmare parenting scenario she was forced into by a rare gene that stole her son's future. She deals with the pain not by lamentation (though there is much of that) but by embracing her literary talents and searching for a new sense of meaning."   —G. Clay Whitaker, *The Daily Beast*

"There are moments in Emily Rapp's memoir *The Still Point of the Turning World* that take us to places language usually cannot reach. . . . Rapp's impassioned, messy, brilliant memoir achieves raw truth by tapping into archetypes that live deep inside us all, buried carefully under layers of defenses that allow most of us to live our day-to-day lives without constant existential and personal crisis. . . . She is, quite simply, an essential writer for *this* world, in which we are all condemned and blessed to live."

—Gina Frangello, Bookslut.com

"Rapp has written a beautiful and passionate elegy for her son, a book that offers deep wisdom for any reader. . . . There are no tidy lessons here, but instead a dark, beautiful sky full of possible constellations of meaning, threads of resonance on the subjects of life, death, healing, illness, friendship, family, grief, and love."   —Buzzy Jackson, *The Boston Globe*

"But [*The Still Point of the Turning World*] is also forceful, inspiring, and filled with lessons for parents. . . . Though her experience is rare, Rapp's ability to translate what happened into lessons for other moms and dads is her gift to us."   —Farah L. Miller, *Huffington Post* Parents

"Rapp is truthful, which makes her story both wrenching and refreshing to read. She shares no platitudes or explanations—just the raw emotions. . . . Emily Rapp's willingness to share these philosophical, emotional, and practical issues makes this book particularly helpful for parents facing similar struggles."   —Marianne Peters, Bookpage.com

"*The Still Point* is a slow burn. . . . There are joys to be found in Rapp's elegant prose."   —Kevin Nguyen, grantland.com

"It's hard to find words that do justice to Emily Rapp's *The Still Point of the Turning World*. It's one of those rare books that you want to press into people's hands and simply say, 'You must read this. You will thank me.' At every turn, Rapp avoids the maudlin and the expected to get at very deep truths, sometimes painful and sometimes liberating and sometimes both. She looks for wisdom and comfort to a wide range of sources ranging from C. S. Lewis to Marilynne Robinson to Buddhist teaching. And she looks to her son. This is one family's story of living while facing death, but also an astonishingly generous work about recognizing the pain and grace that exist all around us."   —Will Schwalbe, *New York Times* bestselling author
of *The End of Your Life Book Club*

"A writer writes; a mother mothers. When those passionate vocations merge in crisis, more than a memoir emerges. *The Still Point of the Turning World* is a philosophical inquiry into the nature of faith, character, love, and dying. This book is Rapp's, and Ronan's, enduring gift of selves for the rest of us."

—Antonya Nelson, author of *Nothing Right* and *Some Fun*

"Written with remarkable precision and restraint, Emily Rapp's *The Still Point of the Turning World* takes us to the depths of grief, where almost against our will, heartbreak becomes beautiful."

—Roger Rosenblatt, author of *Making Toast* and *Kayak Morning*

"I don't know anyone who writes with such clarity and grace about deep sadness and motherlove, about the beauty that is part of the hardest things in life: not transcendent, but quotidian. Rapp's voice is clear-eyed, love-filled, usefully angry, acute, thought-provoking, and tremendously moving. It tries to understand the incomprehensible, to delineate the unimaginable. This is an important book that will mean a great deal to many, many people."

—Elizabeth McCracken, author of *The Giant's House* and
An Exact Replica of a Figment of My Imagination

"Emily Rapp has written an intimate, compelling, and often unexpectedly funny story that speaks to some of the most universal truths of being human. More than just a narrative, this is art, not to mention essential reading."

—Gary Shteyngart, author of *The Russian Debutante's Handbook*,
Absurdistan, and *Super Sad True Love Story*

"Emily Rapp transforms her particular life situation—being a mother to her son Ronan who is dying of Tay-Sachs disease—into something universal, challenging readers to remember that love is all we ever have. Rapp's words will sear your heart and make you want to be a better parent, sister, partner, friend. Reading her book will change your life."

—Sarah Sentilles, author of *Breaking Up with God: A Love Story*

"Emily Rapp vows not to avert her eyes, and she keeps her promise: to the son she is losing to a rare genetic disease, to her family, and to her readers. The result is a staggeringly brilliant and heartbreaking exploration of love, literature, life, death, and belief. Rapp's language is as propulsive and beautiful as her grief is brutal, and her intellectual curiosity is insatiable. She asks the hardest questions any human being is ever forced to ask, about how we understand ourselves and our children, how we love and learn to let each other go. Reading Emily Rapp is like visiting a lush, complicated, inimitable planet. Fly there as fast as you can."

—Rachel Dewoskin, author of *Big Girl Small*, *Foreign Babes
in Beijing*, and *Repeat After Me*

"*The Still Point of the Turning World* is about the smallest things and the biggest things, the ugliest things and the most beautiful things, the darkest things and the brightest things, but most of all it's about one very important thing: the way a woman loves a boy who will soon die. Emily Rapp didn't want to tell us this story. She had to. That necessity is evident in every word of this intelligent, ferocious, grace-filled, gritty, astonishing starlight of a book."

—Cheryl Strayed, author of *Wild*

To access Penguin Readers Guides online,
visit our Web site at www.penguin.com.

THE
STILL
POINT
OF
THE
TURNING
WORLD

Emily Rapp

PENGUIN PRESS

THE PENGUIN PRESS
Published by the Penguin Group
Penguin Group (USA) LLC
375 Hudson Street
New York, New York 10014

USA | Canada | UK | Ireland | Australia | New Zealand | India | South Africa | China
penguin.com
A Penguin Random House Company

First published in the United States of America by The Penguin Press,
a member of Penguin Group (USA) Inc., 2013
Published with a new afterword in Penguin Books 2014

THE LIBRARY OF CONGRESS HAS CATALOGED THE HARDCOVER EDITION AS FOLLOWS:

Rapp, Emily.
The still point of the turning world / Emily Rapp.
pages cm
ISBN 978-1-59420-512-5 (hc.)
ISBN 978-0-14-312510-5 (pbk.)
1. Rapp, Emily—Biography.   2. Tay-Sachs disease—Patients—Biography.   3. Terminally ill
children—Family relationships—Biography.   I. Title.
RJ399.T36R37 2013
618.92'8588450092—dc23
[B]
2012039516

Printed in the United States of America
10 9 8 7 6 5 4 3 2 1

Designed by Marysarah Quinn

FOR RONAN, ALWAYS

I love the handful of earth you are.

—Pablo Neruda,
100 Love Sonnets

1

This is a love story, which, like all great love stories, is ultimately a story of loss. On January 10, 2011, my husband, Rick, and I received the worst possible news: that our son, Ronan, then nine months old, had Tay-Sachs disease, a rare, progressive and always fatal condition with no treatment and no cure.

I had been worried for some time. Ronan was experiencing developmental delays, missing important milestones. I would rush home from work each day hoping he'd started to crawl or had said his first word. He was the same sweet, happy, gurgling baby—but that was the problem. He was the same at nine months old as he had been at six months. Our pediatrician suggested that we rule out any vision problems, so we drove from our home in Santa Fe to the pediatric ophthalmologist's office in Albuquerque.

I sat in the examination chair as the eye doctor, a short, friendly man with black glasses, played cartoons for Ronan on his iPhone and flashed a series of lights in Ronan's eyes. "He's got good fixation," he said. Ronan squirmed in my lap. *Great*, I thought, *he can see.* But behind this feeling of relief was a surge of panic—why, then, was he having these delays? I handed Ronan to Rick and sat in a chair nearby.

"Let me just check his retinas," the doctor said, and hit the lights. I could see Ronan's little eyes flash in the dark, and then Rick's. The doctor carefully approached Ronan and peered into his eyes using a special light.

"Oh, boy," the doctor said. "Oh, boy" was what my father had said when the doctors told my parents about my birth defect, which resulted in the amputation of my left foot. I gripped the sides of the chair and felt the floor drop away. The doctor flipped on the lights and said, "I've only seen this one other time."

"What is it?" I asked, but I could see from his face that it was disastrous.

"Hey, little guy," Rick said, and turned Ronan to face him.

"Rick," I said. My hands were sweating, trembling. "Rick!"

"He has cherry-red spots on the backs of his retinas," the doctor continued. "I've only seen this one other time in fifteen years of practice. It's Tay-Sachs." He paused. "I am so sorry."

"What's that?" Rick asked calmly, but then he quickly had to attend to me because I was wailing. I had wet my pants. The doctor calmly called for a nurse.

"I was tested!" I shouted. "I had the test." I remembered the genetic counselor asking, "Are you Jewish?" and shaking my head. "I want the Tay-Sachs test anyway," I'd said. Or had I? Had I, in this moment, instantly generated a memory to try to mitigate the present horror?

"I don't know," the doctor said uncertainly, and looked as if he might cry. I stared at him. "Did I?" I asked in a squeaky voice, but of course he would not know. He was the eye doctor, a man we'd just met, not the person who had administered the test. He shook his head and cleared his throat. I would later learn that the standard prenatal screening for Tay-Sachs only detects the nine most common mutations—those found among the Ashkenazi Jewish population—but there are more than one hundred known mutations. I would have needed to ask for a combination DNA and enzyme test or requested that my DNA be sequenced. I had not known to ask for either of these. I was told the odds of my being a carrier were "astronomical," and both parents must be carriers for a child to inherit Tay-Sachs. Rick is Jewish, but by testing one of us, we thought we were covering our bases.

"My mom, my mom," I said to Rick, gripping his arm and then taking Ronan from him. I clutched at my son, running my shaking hands over his head, his arms, his fat legs. "Little guy, little guy," I said. He squirmed and giggled. I had the urge to swallow him, to try to return him to my body, where he'd be safe, but of course he'd never been safe, not even there. "Where's my mom?" I was shouting now. "I need to call my mom. Where's the phone? Give me the phone."

"Well, what can we do about it?" Rick asked, glancing between me and Ronan and the doctor, digging in the diaper bag for the cell phone, but I knew enough about Tay-Sachs to know that there was nothing at all for us to do and that my life, the life as a new and hopeful mother, was over.

The doctor looked at the two of us. "No, I'm so sorry," he said. "There's no way to fix it."

"They die," I stuttered. I had the sensation of skin falling away from bone. I hugged Ronan more tightly. "They. Die." I wanted to vomit, and my grip on Ronan was scaring him. I loosened my arms slightly.

"What?" Rick asked. "Surely—"

"They die," I said firmly in a high-pitched voice, and this time he understood that I meant Ronan, that Ronan—our boy, our baby, our child—would die. The world was broken, and the three of us—Ronan, Rick and I—were falling into its mouth

Nerve damage begins in the womb and progresses quickly, leading to dementia, decreased interaction with the environment, seizures, spasticity, and eventually death. Paralysis, blindness, deafness, loss of all faculties. The doctor showed us a laminated medical photograph of normal retinas, and then another set with red spots drawn in the center of diseased retinas, ruined eyes. Another doctor checked Ronan's eyes again, stoically, to confirm the diagnosis. "Yes, I'd agree that it's Tay-Sachs," he said, and quickly left the room.

Hearing these details of Ronan's prognosis, I suddenly, weirdly, remembered meeting a boy called Ronan at Trinity College on a warm, rainy day in Dublin in 1994 and deciding on that name for my future child. I remembered his hand, soft and warm, in my own, and the blond curls that stopped just short of his eyebrows. For years I wrote "Ronan" in longhand scrawls across notebooks like a lovesick teenager, copying over and over again the name, tracing the curved letters as if I were fingering a magic stone. And as if the ghost of Emily Dickinson were speaking directly into my ear, I remembered these lines: *I felt a Cleaving in my Mind / As if my Brain had split. / I tried to match it—Seam by Seam— / But could not make it fit.* The situation didn't fit; it wasn't right. My brain was broken; my heart had stopped. How could I still be alive, in this room, having been given this knowledge? It was grotesque and absurd and could not be happening.

When our son's diagnosis—his death sentence, really—was delivered, I felt all of the known world unraveling, everything splitting apart. The walls of the doctor's office were no longer beige but purple, glittering, melting, closing in. The nurses were like phantoms, moving in and out of the room with paper cups of water and pinkish-white sedatives balanced like little rafts in their palms, promising relief and oblivion, trying not to stare but staring, whispering *Take this. It will help you relax and calm down.* My voice: not mine. The chairs were a dazzling, terrifying blue and had moved across the room. I was standing on my heart, which was simultaneously beating in my nose. I had finally reached my mother on the phone and was screaming at her but no words left my mouth. My hair was on fire but my face was cold. I had swallowed my own teeth. *What do you mean there's nothing to do? Are you sure? I can't believe there's nothing we can do,* Rick was saying. Action was required, it seemed, but action was useless.

Yet in my blown-apart mind I was already brokering a deal. *If you take Tay-Sachs from Ronan, I will do anything you ask. I'll stick a knife in anyone's heart, kill any person, just say the word.* Jesus, Zeus, God, G-d, Allah, anyone. Useless bargaining with a higher power I had long ago stopped believing in. To my own horror, I prayed as I had as a child in church, as I had as a young theologian in divinity school, and I was so overwhelmed, so out of my body, so fully in the dream of disbelief, that I actually believed for a moment that it might work.

"Whatever we can do," the doctor said in a barely controlled voice. "You just let us know." But what could he—or we—do? There was nothing to do. He filled our heads with more information—names of doctors, specialists, geneticists—while Rick and I sat on uncomfortable chairs and clung to each other in the overheated, badly lit room, repeating each other's first names.

Finally, with Ronan carried between us in his car seat, we stumbled out of the examination room as if groping our way through a dark tunnel instead of the well-lit hallway.

"Why is the floor wet?" I asked Rick. Ronan gurgled and burped in his car seat.

"It isn't," he said. "It's carpeted. This is carpet."

"Be careful," I insisted. "Don't slip. Don't drop the baby!"

"I've got him. I'm fine. It's fine."

"Take care," the nurses said with trembling voices as we passed their station.

Riding home in the backseat, clutching at my kid, who sat giggling in his car seat, oblivious to his wretched future, I thought *I can't believe I'm awake for this. I don't want to be awake for this.*

I was filled with a pulse-pounding terror, a wrenching euphoria of disbelief. My chest was hot, liquid and loud with fear. I felt gleaming and flattened. *I'm sure I had the test for Tay-Sachs,* I reminded myself. *It's a mistake; it must be.* The cars on the highway looked as real to me as those on *The Jetsons*. My parents were already on their way from Cheyenne, Wyoming, to Santa Fe, a seven-hour drive, and I called them nearly every ten minutes until they arrived, when I stumbled, wailing, into my mother's arms, sedated but still writhing, out of time and feverish with panic and fear. I repeated "blackness," over and over again, and I could feel it descending. I put my hands over my head as if to shield myself. I called my closest friends and screamed and wept into the phone. *I'm here,* they promised. *I'll leave the phone on, I'll book a ticket, tell me what I can do.*

I couldn't eat or think, and when I moved, I paced back and forth in my room. I threw a chair at the wall and kicked it with my bare foot. I knelt on the floor and hit my head against the wood until Rick pulled me up, and then I hit my head against the wall. Rick and I met with Matt, the chairman of my department at the arts school where I teach writing and literature, but I remember very little about the conversation, only that as I watched Rick explain to him why I wouldn't be able to teach

for the next few weeks, and struggling not to cry, I was thinking of friends who had lost parents and children, and I kept
asking Rick, again, if I could use his phone. *I have to call them,* I
pleaded, clawing at his jacket. *And tell them that I know their hearts,
that I know them now.* And then, finally, I slept.

As news of Ronan's diagnosis spread, our house on Sol y Luz
Street, "street of sun and light," in Santa Fe became a busy
place, its own little planet. Baskets of food arrived at our door.
Phone calls poured in. My friend Emily booked a ticket from
London to arrive in a matter of days. A constant flurry of
e-mails began, which I checked compulsively, as if sending
e-mails like a normal, functional person would save me from
facing reality. I nibbled at some Danish that my friends Lisa
and David had sent from Los Angeles. My friend Tara called
me every hour from Phoenix.

I took Ronan for a walk in his front carrier pack, crying
behind a pair of diva sunglasses. I stopped wailing, except at
night, when I would cry myself into a pit and then sleep there,
shallowly. When I woke up, I felt as if I'd spent the night in a
cold, skinny ditch by the side of some lonely road. Every morning the sky was bright blue and mocking, the trees along the
walking trail outside our house still bare, everything brown.
The world blue-brown but black, like a bruise. We felt beat up,
pressed down. The world had a wild, new, terrifying clarity. I
thought of these lines from "The Elm," by Sylvia Plath: *Now I*

break up in pieces that fly about like clubs / A wind of such violence / Will tolerate no bystanding: I must shriek. They repeated over and over again in my head like a ticker tape, like a mantra, like a warning from a future haunted version of myself.

In Boston my friend Weber went online and found the National Tay-Sachs and Allied Diseases Association and joined on our family's behalf. Mothers of children who had died of Tay-Sachs started calling me from phone numbers and area codes I didn't recognize—moms from Florida, New York, New Jersey, California. I talked with them for hours, in my bed and under the covers with Ronan, sweating, clinging to my son. I learned details of what his care would entail: head supports, bath chairs, seizure medications, suction machines. I clung to one mom's description that Tay-Sachs would function like a "slow fade" and that Ronan would not be in pain. It felt strange to be sharing, suddenly, such a life-altering experience—the very worst experience—with people I hardly knew. I appreciated that this dynamic meant that all the usual formalities disappeared. Instead it was *what do you want to know* and *you are not alone* and *yes, there's hope for future children* and *it is the worst thing you will ever experience and you will survive if not ever fully recover* and *you call me anytime and ask me any question and I will tell you the truth and I am here.* No platitudes ("What doesn't kill you will make you stronger!"), no annoying, schmaltzy pseudo-Christian phrases like "When God closes a door, he opens a window."

Weber gently asked if I planned to write about Ronan. "Uh . . . I don't know . . . maybe." I stuttered. "I'll set up a blog space," she said. "You can always decide later." I didn't think much about it at the time. I talked to the other moms with terminally ill babies, I took Xanax, I sobbed and bit my lip, my sheets, my hands. And then I got out of bed, and, to my great surprise, I started to write.

2

You feel your obligation to a child when
you have seen it and held it. Any human
face is a claim on you, because you can't
help but understand the singularity of it,
the courage and loneliness of it. But this
is truest of the face of an infant. I consider
that to be one kind of vision, as mystical
as any.

—Marilynne Robinson, *Gilead*

What could I say about my son, about being a mom in
the wake of Ronan's diagnosis? What had I, in just a
few short days, learned from the other moms parenting children with Tay-Sachs or similar diseases? How do you parent
without a future, knowing that you will lose your child, bit by
torturous bit? Could it even be called parenting, or was it something else, and if so, what? As I sat down to write, I bristled at

the lack of information and resources for parents who are not concerned with whether or not their children will be admitted to Harvard or win prizes for piano performances or even be productive and gracious or successful in school, but are instead involved in the daily grind of making the short lives of their children as full as possible for two, three, maybe six years at the outward reach, depending on how the disease progresses and the levels of medical intervention. *What will I read?* I wondered as I tossed out all the old guides about what to expect, all the old developmental charts. For parents of terminally ill children, parenting strategies incorporate the grim reality that we will not be launching our children into a bright and promising future, but into early graves. The goals for our children are simple and terrible and absolutely grounded in the everyday: dignity and minimal discomfort.

This was absolutely depressing. The moms I talked to were very honest about the horror of what was coming for me. But the experience of being Ronan's mom was not, I grew to learn, without wisdom, not without—forced and unwelcome as it might be to those of us going through it—a profound understanding of the human experience, which includes the reality of death in life that most parenting books and resources fail to acknowledge. Parents with dying kids have insights into parenting and they are hard-won, forged through the prism of hellish grief and helplessness and deeply committed love. These women had learned lessons not just about how to be a mother but how to be *human*.

But parenting for the sake of parenting, for the ancient humanity implicit in the act itself, appeared to contradict every bit of parenting advice I'd ever read, having devoured the magazines while I was pregnant and then as a new mom. The task of parenting seemed to have evolved from "do your best to keep your baby alive," which was the primary parenting goal even into the nineteenth century, to the challenge presented to modern parents to "make sure your kid is prepped from the outset with the tools (here they are, and here are the studies that prove the worth of these expensive strollers, special bottles, organic cotton clothes, well-known tutors, popular programs, et cetera) that will lead to acceptance into the best preschool, the best grade school, high school, college, which will in turn lead to the best partner, résumé, job, bank account, *life*. The demand for these Olympic efforts presumes an implicit—and erroneous—belief that any parent can fully control a child's destiny. Moms and dads in Victorian London were more concerned with mundane issues like cleanliness and making sure their kid didn't catch a potentially fatal sickness from the dirty, teeming streets. This is still a real concern for parents in much of the world.

Parenting advice is, by its very nature, future directed. I learned to avoid the magazines in the pediatrician's office that were full of articles about optimizing a child's sensory and language experiences in order to fire the right cerebral neurons; cures for colic; the politics of playdates; clothing "lines" endorsed by this or that ridiculous celebrity spokesmom.

Future, future, future. During this time, just before I boycotted parenting magazines, I came upon this quiz in a popular magazine that was marketed for people of my age, educational level and "life stage":

What's the hardest challenge for parents today?

~ Supervising cell phone and Internet use
~ Kids' friends raised in more permissive homes
~ Helping kids deal with more tests and pressure in school
~ Kids today are growing up too fast!

Here's how the options might read for the parent of a child with Tay-Sachs or another terminal illness:

~ Waking up every morning dreading the next stage of this disease (paralysis, blindness, deafness, spasticity, seizures, death)
~ Learning who your friends are, and how sickness makes people uncomfortable
~ INSURANCE
~ Kids with Tay-Sachs will never grow up!

But in the months following Ronan's diagnosis, after the initial shock had worn off, the day-to-day routine with Ronan was peaceful. A typical day included cuddling, feedings, naps. He had water therapy and acupuncture. I worked during his naps. There was a baby dinner (peas!), bath-bottle-sleep, dinner for adults (takeout). Not so atypical of a family juggling schedules and running a typical baby day. We did our best for our kid, fed him fresh food, brushed his teeth, made sure he was clean and warm and well rested and . . . healthy?

Well, no. The dreadful hitch in this otherwise middle-class and privileged domestic snapshot was this: Ronan would never benefit from any of Rick's and my efforts beyond what he received *in the moment.* I told him I loved him and so did his father, even if Ronan never understood the words. I encouraged Ronan to do what he could, although he was without ego or ambition. Babies aren't investments that accrue interest. They're not stocks or bonds or diversified portfolios to be reorganized in "these tough economic times." They're people, and, like all people, they can and will eventually die.

I didn't always think like this. During my pregnancy and throughout those first nine months of Ronan's life, I devised an ambitious list that I hoped would lead to important development outcomes for him: I would talk to him in different languages (language development); pick him up when he cried (attachment issues are crucial in the first year of life); breastfeed exclusively for a properly developing brain (I took herculean and often expensive and painful measures to do this). Like his father he would complete crossword puzzles in record time. Like me he would be physically fearless and an adventurous eater. He'd be fun but levelheaded, loyal and fair and smart. I would teach him how to ski and read and travel on a bare-bones budget. Maybe he would invent something world changing or build space rockets or become a fashion designer who made clothes from recycled trash. He would be generous and gorgeous. Women or men would be falling all over themselves to go out with him. I was not above my own prodigy dreams.

But no matter what I did for Ronan—organic or nonorganic food; cloth or disposable diapers; attachment parenting or sleep training; breast milk or formula—all decisions that mattered *so much* to me in the first few months of his life, he was going to die. End of story. Or was it? As I pondered these questions in the early hours of the morning and late hours of the night, I began to understand that the story of my son's life would end but that what he had to teach me was as epic and mythic as a creation story. To prepare throughout a child's whole life for the loss of that boy or that girl, and then to live with it, takes a new ferocity, a new way of thinking, a new animal.

What creature symbolized this modern love story of which Ronan and Rick and I and others were a part but whose roots were as ancient and mysterious as the Tay-Sachs gene itself? What could represent us, we parents who learned how to use suction machines, clean catheters and feeding tubes, operate oxygen tanks, navigate weird insurance phone trees and manage the prejudices of others in order to be sure our children were comfortable, loved, and stayed in the world for as long as they could? Who were these moms who answered all manner of rude questions in grocery stores ("What's wrong with your baby?" or "How can you drag that child all around town when he looks so tired?") and who were confronted with unsolicited statements like "I hope you got sterilized" or "Why didn't you get tested if you knew it was genetic?" or "I didn't know you were Jewish" and other statements that speak to ignorance and exhibit basic cruelty?

The English word "dragon" is derived from the Greek verb "to see clearly." Dragons are creatures of myth and legend, beasts with the magical power of unicorns but made of much tougher, less ethereal stuff.

What I came to understand was that mothers and fathers who take on the qualities of dragons feel as though parenting were our only task, and yet none of the parenting resources were written for us. Parenting books revolve around the issues that arise from children who grow, wreak havoc, talk back, succeed, do drugs, overcome learning obstacles. Of course, parenting books are designed for parents with children who live, but dragon parents have a lot to say about parenting. Why? Because we've had to redefine the act: parenting with no thought to that dreaded future when there will be no child—parenting without a net.

"You must be so proud" is the kind of thing all parents are fond of saying to one another. Yes, my parents are proud of me. But as I thought about Ronan, I wondered: under what circumstances would it have been appropriate or acceptable for them to be less proud? If I'd never done anything "prideworthy," would people have avoided talking about me with my parents at all? If I'd robbed a bank or run someone down with my car while driving drunk, would people have pretended as though I didn't exist? I was proud of Ronan, but not for anything he did or for any future accolade, and that was not easy. I was not above the petty stuff.

I realized that it was very likely that had it not been for Ronan's terminal diagnosis, I'd still be living out these old stories through my unsuspecting son. It took this experience to help me see clearly, to understand that the bulk of the popular parenting advice champions an approach to living that completely complies with achieving bogus standards of success, but it didn't mean I was immune to the longing for those meaningless benchmarks. Still, I felt as if discussions about "taking pride in our children" implied that they'd better earn their keep, that they'd better deserve all the attention and privileges provided for them. Dragons might be associated with medieval myth and ancient legend, but this very modern parenting practice seemed straight out of the Dark Ages—punitive and transactional and cruel.

Why are mothers of terminally ill children rarely asked for their parenting views?

Short answer: dragons are scary. Our grief is primal and unwieldy and it embarrasses people. Talking about end-of-life care decisions for our babies to a bunch of parents with typically developing kids is tantamount to breathing fire at a dinner party or on the playground. Nobody wants to see what we see so clearly. Nobody wants to know the truth about their children, about themselves: that none of it is forever.

Dragons are descended from serpents and dinosaurs, winged in some cultures, reptilian in others. We have an underappreciated ability to force people to face their worst fears. Our scales act like mirrors and our news looks dreadful. We foretell disaster. We don't fit in normal-sized rooms. We lament. We gather in underground lairs. We fly loudly and awkwardly and in smelly, loyal packs. Our narratives are grisly and the stakes are impossibly high. And there's this: maybe for parents who, in this day and age and particularly in this country, seem expected to be *super*human, nobody wants to listen to insights into the human condition, all of which end with one result—death.

"Here be dragons" was an ancient cartographer's way of marking new territories that were unknown and therefore considered dangerous. Medieval mapmakers sketched dragons into those blank spaces as a warning. Dragon mothers are navigating these unchartered parenting waters, terrified, but without another choice.

We bellow and bark and roar, but we can also dance, as I once saw a dragon do through the steamy streets of Hong Kong in the summer of 1997. We watch our children carefully, vigilantly, breathing softly over them like dragons of old guarding their treasures. We can laugh, cry, sing, get drunk, *live*. Remember Puff and Jackie Paper? We can frolic in the mist. We are gentle and loving and kind. Dragons live forever, but not so boys and girls. We dragon mothers know this better than most, and while we will not live forever, we *will* live for the rest of our lives with a great big hole blown through our hearts. To endure this requires a barbaric strength (and I don't mean the kind that dictates the pulling of privileged strings, the hounding, the hovering, the pushing) and a ridiculous amount of grace and humor. Great strength combined with a raw vulnerability: the ultimate expression of power.

I wasn't interested in music class and swimming lessons for Ronan because I hoped he would manifest some fabulous talent that would set him, and therefore *me*, apart. I wasn't searching for heaps of praise about what an amazing mom I was. I was interested in creating experiences for Ronan that would make him *happy*. I protected Ronan from what I could. I brushed his teeth to keep them from rotting even though he never chewed solid food. I fed him, held him, rocked him to sleep. I was being asked to remember even when I wanted to forget.

Most important, Ronan taught me that children do not exist to honor their parents; their parents exist to honor them. My time with Ronan was short and beautiful and shot through with light, laughter and, above all, a kind of love that stripped me to the bone. A magical world, yes, where there were no goals, no prizes to win, no outcomes to monitor. Ronan was given a terrible freedom from those expectations that was searing, brutal and, especially, *true*. Ronan was mine but he never belonged to me. This was not an issue of ownership. A child is not a couch.

Was the care I gave Ronan "worth it"? He would never come sprinting at me with a Harvard diploma in his hand. He would never score a perfect SAT. He never said "mama." He never knew about 9/11 and other catastrophic events that happened all over the world. He would never go to war. He never knew any wickedness at all. That was my role as a dragon mother, as it is for others: to protect my child from wickedness and as much suffering as possible and then, finally, to do the hardest thing of all, a thing most parents will thankfully never have to do: let him go.

Agony is not an experience that's easy to describe. How could I write the story of Ronan's life? How could I create order from chaos and find underlying patterns of meaning in a situation that, from the outside, looked inviolate and incontrovertibly meaningless? I came up violently short. The narrative was empty. What could I say? Even with the image of the dragon in my mind, I felt hollowness, that familiar blackness, and the desire to crawl out of my own skin. I sat in front of the computer and typed Ronan's name over and over again while listening to see if he was stirring in his crib. But I am a writer. I write. And just as I had written through every experience, euphoric or horrific, throughout my life, I began to document the daily happenings of my son's short life. Once I started I didn't—I couldn't—stop.

Ronan was born in March 2010 and spent his first nights wrapped up like a burrito in the clear plastic crib next to my hospital bed at Cedars-Sinai Medical Center in Los Angeles. Ronan made me happy then, long before the dread associated with his progressive illness, and he made me happy every day after his terminal diagnosis with his round face and green-gold-brown-yellow eyes; his perfect toes; his fat ankles; his pointed boy-ballerina feet; his impossibly long, pale eyelashes; his sticky, sweaty hands; his long contented sighs; the soft angle of his nose; the way he made an *oh-no-this-might-be-gross* face when he tasted his first spoonful of solid food, even if it was his fa-vorite (avocado); the duck tail of wavy hair at the back of his head that bounced into ringlets at the first touch of humidity in the air; the way he'd sit on my lap and then suddenly look at me and smile as if he'd just realized—*Ah! Here you are!*—that I'd arrived. I loved his contemplative looks, his grumpy glares, his well-timed sighs. I loved the way he held up his hand and waved his fingers at himself, marveling, as if to ask, *Are these really mine?* I loved the way his soft body floated in the therapy pool, a tiny merman, his wet curls trailing behind him like seaweed. And later, when he became more withdrawn, I loved the look of his eyes blinking in the light, although he could no longer see, and the sudden coo and wiggle as he sat next to me on the couch listening to opera, sleeping side by side with him, his forehead pressed to mine. I loved the look of his wet face in the bathtub, his feet dangling in the warm water, his soft and flawless skin. Held in this happiness, of course, was the knowl-edge that any smile might be the last one, and that even before his biggest period of regression he was already irretrievably and heartbreakingly lost. Tucked inside the moments of this great sadness—this feeling of being punctured, scrambling and

stricken—were also moments of the brightest, most swollen
and logic-shattering happiness I've ever experienced. One moment would be a wall of happiness so tall it could not be scaled;
the next felt like falling into a pit of sadness that had no bottom. I realized you could not have one without the other, that
this great capacity to love and be happy can be experienced only
with this great risk of having happiness taken from you—to
tremble, always, on the edge of loss.

We know that everyone we love will change and all of them
will die, but it's harder to fully accept this knowledge while
holding a sick baby, especially when that baby is yours. The
acceptance was a daily challenge, like attempting each day to
escape from a prison even though you know your efforts will be
fruitless.

I was and have been many things—a writer, a wife, a friend,
a teacher, a lover, a sister, a niece, a daughter, a skeptic, a former
Christian, an itinerant theologian—but since January 10, 2011,
I have been one thing in particular: Ronan's mom. The more I
wrote about Ronan, the more I understood that the only way
grief would not take me down completely was to greet his diagnosis head-on and make my world big, make his story known.
His myth is an account of loving and letting go, it's about art
and literature and movies, about theology and philosophy and
animals. It is about the joys and costs of refusing to look away,
of diving into the abyss and kicking around in it, about going
forward in life even though there is no sign that things will
change or be solved or get better.

Akira Kurosawa once said that "to be an artist means never to avert one's eyes." I read this in *From Where You Dream*, Robert Olen Butler's book about crafting fiction, on a plane from Los Angeles to Santa Fe the day before Ronan's diagnosis, when I still cared about pursuing a life of art—things that mattered no longer in the days that followed, and then quickly began to matter to me more than they ever had before. I was reminded of Kurosawa's words on "diagnosis day" as we discussed Ronan's prognosis with doctors and specialists who poked and prodded and examined him and stretched a rubber band across his forehead like a mean-spirited halo in order to draw blood from a vein. "Prognosis," a word cut from metal, from iron, a word with the sharpest edges.

On January 10, Rick and I did not know the full details of what lay ahead, only that it would be the most difficult test of our lives. There is no cure for Tay-Sachs, no arguing with biology. We understood that our son would gradually regress into a vegetative state within the span of one year, and that this slow fade would progress to his likely death before the age of three. He would slowly go blind. He would never speak or walk and he would lose control over his head and never have control over any other part of his body. We understood that we would suffer as he withdrew, as he changed, as his interaction with us diminished, but because we were his parents, we were determined to make each remaining moment of his life one touched by love.

As tragic as the situation appeared from the outside, the

inside of our lives was often blissful, despite the daily very real dread about what was happening as this ridiculous disease spread across Ronan's brain and shut down his body. In the morning we lifted Ronan from his crib and kissed him. There was joy. We laughed. We lived. I took him hiking and rubbed his fat feet in the dirt and lifted his face to the juniper-scented breeze. He went on road trips, to parties, coffee shops and restaurants. He was our companion, our child, our beloved.

3

It is the part of the journey where the
staircase gets narrow and you must turn
sideways to pass.

—Tony Hoagland, "LOVE"

When I was growing up, there was a giant dollhouse in the lobby of the Denver Children's Hospital. My small dollhouse at home had white walls and rickety furniture, but these rooms were elaborately decorated. The red wallpaper in the living room was striped with delicate gold. Tiny chandeliers glimmered from the ceilings. A pink canopy bed in the corner of one bedroom looked as sweet as wrapped candy, and a white bassinet sat near the window in the baby's room. I remember thinking that the doorways were tall enough that I might actually fit inside—but the house was surrounded by glass. It was tantalizingly perfect, but impossible.

I was a frequent patient there. Because of a congenital birth defect, my left foot had been amputated when I was four; this was followed by endless X-rays, prosthetic leg fittings and consultations with my orthopedic surgeon. After these humiliating and occasionally painful appointments, I insisted that my mother leave me alone for a bit with the dollhouse. I circled it, watching my reflection in the smudged glass move over those beautifully appointed rooms. I longed to be small enough to sprawl on the shiny patterned chaise lounges in the living room with its oval mirror and polished lamps, or to sit down for dinner at the table with its silver forks and gleaming white plates. During the holidays (when I was often back in the hospital for more surgery), a fake Christmas tree glittered in the corner, garlanded with popcorn strings and sequined ornaments and with miniature wrapped presents stacked underneath. Life inside the dollhouse was the antidote to life at the hospital, infused with soft light, perfect and contained, procedure-free and comfortable. *Someday,* I thought, *I'll live in a house like this, and everything will finally be set right.*

The notion that happiness and fulfillment hinge upon radical transformation followed me throughout my life. From an early age, I had fantasies of being "healed" of my disability, a miracle I envisioned as rather more Disney than biblical. As my body levitated from the bed in a haze of glitter, my hair, spun in a French twist, would sparkle. My skin would shine. Free of my wooden leg and the need for it, ball gown spinning out around me, my perfect body would land in an adult-sized version of that dollhouse along with my adult-sized husband (attractive and successful) and slightly smaller children (brilliant and Ivy League bound). I would effortlessly serve elaborate dinner parties, be the perfect mother and write a best-selling novel every month. I would finally be at home.

I was born in Nebraska, and one morning when I was four years old my mom was out on the porch with me when a woman walking by on the street approached her and started asking questions: "What's wrong with your baby? How come she looks that way?" I had just been fitted with my first wooden leg—a scary-looking contraption made of cloth, metal and wood, a leg right out of the Iron Age, but circa the late 1970s, in this case. (People are often shocked at or even disbelieving of the rudimentary technology of my first legs. My parents were simply offered what they were told was available, and they accepted it.) My mom told this passerby about my disability and she replied, "Well, I guess you can love her anyway, even if she only has one leg." My mom was angry, naturally, but at this time she was not yet comfortable with being confrontational. Instead, she hauled me inside, wooden leg and all, and loved me. She never stopped.

One of the hardest parts of living with a disability is dealing with other people's responses to it. People often find this baffling. *Don't you wish you could just have two legs?* Yes, it would be easier, but it's impossible, and this body is what I've always known. It would be nice, however, to move through the world without people assuming that when you are disabled, the devastation is constant, total, consuming and ever present. It isn't.

But if you fall too far outside culture's ridiculously restrictive assumptions about what a "good" body looks like and does, people believe that one quick glance is enough to pass judgment on your quality of life, your prospects, perhaps even your state of mind and your basic goodness. I've been both pitied and admired because I wear an artificial leg, and it's sometimes difficult to decide which is worse. Some examples: "If I had one leg, I'd never leave the house!" Really? That seems impractical. "I can't imagine how you live." Day by day, just like everybody else. "You are so brave and amazing." What would make us hibernate, as people with disabilities, what would make us hide? Why this shame that grips and won't let go? Why this idea that people with disabilities are "extraordinary" when they are only trying to live ordinary lives? I crossed continents—Africa, Asia, Europe—to try to find answers to these questions.

What I realized was that people across this country and across the world suffer from a lack of imagination when it comes to disability. Disability lacks a frame. We get no assistance from the media, literature and popular culture, where the stories are either full of pity and sadness or impossible physical feats performed by inspiring people with disabilities who run marathons or climb mountains using expensive prosthetic equipment. Most disturbing of all is a common reaction that is rarely questioned: what people view as the "tragedies" of others makes them feel better about themselves. If somebody else has it worse than you, you can walk around feeling lucky for a few minutes. In the weeks following Ronan's diagnosis it upset me to think that Ronan and I had no purpose at all in this world other than to serve as reflections for situations other people feared.

When I was younger, I, too, played this "I'm lucky and you're not" game. I wasn't immune to ranking myself on an unseen ladder of luck, which in some ways, according to my skewed (but common) logic was somehow equated with goodness.

One example: I learned to ski when I was six, at Winter Park in Colorado, at a center built and staffed and funded specifically to teach kids like me to enjoy the best sport in the world (I am admittedly biased). No matter your individual physical or mental limitations, someone could teach you to successfully and safely (well, sort of) fly down a mountain at varying speeds.

Once, when I was a teenager, during a lesson with Dan, my favorite instructor, I said, "I'm so glad I'm not blind. That would be, like, so much worse than having one leg." I don't remember what prompted me to even think this, let alone say it out loud, but when Dan looked at me, I knew I'd said the wrong thing.

"You think?" he asked, knocking one of his poles against my single boot. "You think there's some kind of ranking system, Rapp?" We were midway down a difficult slope, and I'd fallen pretty hard near a line of trees marking the run's edge.

"Uh, I don't know," I said, embarrassed now as I hauled myself up out of the snow, but thinking, *Yeah, you butthead, there is. And I'm at the top of the ladder; I can hide my disability.* And hide it

I did, in some cringe-worthy outfits (think pale blue, high-waisted parachute pants and a matching sweater). I was also thirteen, so a crisis for me might have been an inability to roll up my acid-washed jeans exactly the way my friends did, or glancing in my locker mirror to realize that my side ponytail was tilted at the "wrong" angle, or suffering in my long pants during the summer because I was afraid to be stared at in shorts. And hello? Didn't everything have a ranking system? Every year the junior high yearbook staff handed out awards for best smile (which I *won*, dude, I wanted to say), best personal style, best laugh, et cetera. Dan was a total dweeb! What did he know?

"Do you want to see what it might be like?" he asked. "To ski blind?"

I most certainly did not. A blind skier is tethered with a rope to a skier who moves behind her or him, calling out when to turn; the blind skier has to trust the calls and move left or right when told.

"We'll tree ski," he announced. "It won't be exactly the same thing but it will give you an idea. You'll be able to see, but it won't be easy."

"Isn't that, like, not allowed?" I asked. "Isn't it, like, totally dangerous?"

"Are you going to tell someone?" I was not.

"You have to keep your wits about you," he warned as he skied toward a gap in the trees. "And don't second-guess; just do what I tell you."

I'd never been very good at that. I agreed anyway.

Tree skiing was an absolutely euphoric experience that I will never repeat. There were impossibly tight turns on a steep slope, some ducking involved and sharp tree branches perilously close to my face. The shade from the trees made everything darker, icier. I could feel my heartbeat in my eyeballs. The experience of trusting someone to mark my moves for me as I hurtled down a hill at a terrifying clip was a completely counterintuitive experience. There was no sense of control. Dan would call out "left" when I thought for sure he was about to say "right," and he cut me zero slack. He went *fast*. The experience wasn't worse or better than skiing on one leg; it was just different. Maybe Dan was rash and irresponsible to challenge me on that day, although now I think he did me a favor by teaching me an important lesson about the value of specific experience, the value of individual bodies. It was a lesson I continued to learn as Ronan's mom.

Disabled people are like immigrants wherever we go, routinely asked to justify the landscape of our bodies to people who've never been there or imagined it only in a limited way, through the disability tourism of old stories propagated in literature and movies and news stories—so the question becomes not *Where are you from originally?* but instead *What are you and why?*

When you've got a visible disability or if you're the parent of a disabled child, I quickly learned, your story is up for grabs. People lose track of their manners like coins spilling out of holey pockets, like the string of a kite slipping from a hand.

Although I didn't realize this as a child, wandering around that dollhouse in the children's hospital lobby was about a desire to enclose myself in a compact, sleek, organized, predictable life. Sterile and clean. No chaos, no difference, no mess.

As the mother of a little boy with Tay-Sachs, quite possibly the shittiest disease of all time (as one dragon mom put it, "They never had a chance"), the question "What happened to your baby?" came right after "What happened to you?" It was enough to make me never want to leave the house. But leave it I did. I'd learned to move around in the world, even if it made people uncomfortable, and even if it made me feel vulnerable and raw, bright and strange. Ronan helped teach me a lesson I had long been resisting: this world belongs to everyone. We all have a place in it, no matter how long we live and no matter what we look like, how we move or don't move, how we exist. What matters is that we lived.

Life is challenging for everyone in different ways. Certainly, living with a disability and being the parent of a terminally ill child are both extraordinarily difficult in ways that are probably impossible to imagine for people who haven't experienced them. But it is not all pain and moaning and suffering, and I learned this, too, through the years before I became a mother and then later as Ronan's mom. People assume that you *are* your disability; that you must spend all day bemoaning your fate. Yes, that happens—but it also happens to plenty of non-disabled people. Ronan was Ronan—he was never just a sick baby—and my life as his mother was more than just managing the illness and the many difficulties it presented. The late Czech writer Václav Havel, who was imprisoned for four years of hard labor for his involvement in his country's civil rights movement, said it perfectly in a November 1980 letter to his wife, Olga, in which he compares the loss of a limb to the loss of freedom in prison:

> If you were to spend several years brooding constantly over whom you might be with, where you might be, what you might be doing, eating, etc., if you were free, it would probably drive you mad . . . you focus on values that are within reach: a moment's peace and quiet, time to read something good, a good night's sleep, steering clear of some pointless annoyance, keeping your things clean and neat, satisfaction with your work, etc. While the comparison is not exact (I won't be here for life, I hope), in some ways it's like the condition of the man who loses a leg: as time goes by, he will focus more and more on the best way to walk painlessly with an artificial limb, and less and less on what he might have done if he still had both legs. Yet "two-leggedness" is still a presence in his life, though in a form somewhat different from what it would be in people who actually have two legs. From a fact he takes for granted, it becomes something at once more abstract and more on his mind, the measure of everything he

does—but chiefly the measure of his effort to live with an artificial leg.

The most interesting and perhaps illuminating aspect of Havel's insights as applied to Ronan's situation was that Ronan never had to measure his effort at anything, or take anything for granted, or view himself from the outside in this philosophical way. He never circled a place or the idea of a place, or wondered about his role in it, or whether or not he belonged. He was mercifully free of this thinking; it had, however, helped me to make sense of my own experience of being his mother. For Ronan there was no sense to be made, no change to seek out, no potential to actualize. His life was a collection of singular, unrepeatable moments that were not analyzed, remembered or regretted. What a relief for him and for me.

"I could never do what you do." "I don't know how you cope!" "He is the definition of heartbreak." These are, at their base, simpleminded, misguided and, of course, quite rude remarks, not to mention shortsighted and stupid. Nobody is immune to disease or sickness or any other catastrophic event, and we are all just a disease, a decade, an accident away from disability. So we're afraid. Confronted suddenly with an experience interpreted as tragic and world-ending, people feel helpless and stumble over their words. The death of a baby seems to go against nature, against the advertisements on television about the miracle of birth and the unadulterated joys of parenting, against our hopeful delusion that being good people might keep chaos at bay. But chaos finds everyone, or as the philosopher Ziusudra mourned in 2700 BCE: "Fate is a wet bank, my friends. Sooner or later it will make you slip."

We all want to believe that we're on solid ground and that we won't be the ones to tumble into the mud. But we will. Of course, spouting the existential ponderings of an ancient Sumerian or a dissident writer might be a bit much for the supermarket checkout line or even among a group of artists, intellectuals or writers who are supposed to be thinking on a less quotidian level. We all want to feel in control of our destinies, our wishes and desires; we crave the illusion of control.

In ten years we will have the sequenced genome. We will believe that it is possible to know everything there is to know about who and what we are and adjust expectations and outcomes accordingly. Maybe our genetic material will be included in online dating profiles. Maybe I'll be able to sit on a couch and ask the people sitting opposite me in leather chairs which diseases they carry (because all of us carry something) and which ailments they will likely develop (state the odds, please, for effect) when they age. Maybe I'll ask, *How can you possibly live while carrying around such unfortunate genetics?* We think we will know how to eliminate risk and illuminate only possibility. We believe we'll be able to see everyone from the inside out. We'll be shining our flashlights into one another's mouths, probing for a look, for some great Truth. Will we really want to look? Is that how we want to be known?

We Americans thrive on notions of self-improvement and transformation; we believe this is part of our national ethos and are befuddled by situations that defy solutions. But as those of us who have or have had sick kids know, some situations can't be fixed. Instead they must be borne in whatever ways we can manage. I decided that I was not responsible for managing other people's rude reactions or misconceptions. I was unable to mitigate other people's fears, but I could certainly love Ronan. That was my only job. Babies with disorders like Tay-Sachs don't care about perception, or measuring up, or looking a particular way. I tried to remember this when people stared at Ronan. His experience of being different was *not* mine, and it did, in fact, force me to rethink my own coping strategies, my own lifelong neuroses, my own obsession with being one of the "normal" pack, finding a place, a way to be, a home.

My real-life search for home was exhaustive and nomadic, spanning numerous cities and countries, houses and apartments, jobs and relationships. It took years, but by the time I arrived in Santa Fe in the summer of 2010, I thought I had finally figured it out. I had a steady teaching job, a slew of terrific and loyal friends, and a family. I had my beautiful son, who was then five months old. That first night in Santa Fe, after Ronan was asleep, I lay in bed and watched monsoon rain waterfall over my window and listened to thunder pummeling the seemingly endless New Mexico sky. I remembered that silly dollhouse dream as I had so often over the years and thought: *This is even better.*

When Ronan was newly born, a friend of ours asked, "Isn't it interesting that, of all of us, Ronan has the most life ahead of him and yet he's the least worried about it?" The first part turned out not to be true, of course. Ronan's life would be short—but he would never worry about its length or quality. He would never feel shame, fear or regret. He would never hate himself or his parents. He would find nobody to blame. He would never sit and stare at a house inside a glass box and wish for his life to be different; he would just live it. He would always be at home in his body, the only one he knew, a body he didn't question. He was always, without any effort, at home in the world.

Our home, our life with Ronan, was not the definition of heartbreak. It was, to put it bluntly, the truth about life: that it exists side by side with death. Other cultures and traditions are acutely aware of this intimate pairing. In 1996, as a Fulbright scholar in Seoul, I celebrated the autumn festival of Chusok with my host family at a raucous, boozy party at the family grave plot, complete with music and the favorite foods and drinks of the departed. In one Día de los Muertos image from Mexico, images that are plentiful in Santa Fe, a robust, rosy-cheeked man walks with his skeleton rattling in his arms. One fall afternoon before his terminal diagnosis, I walked with Ronan on the arroyo path near our house, his smiling face peeking up at me from the front pack, the last of the day's sun warm on my shoulders, the mountains darkening to purple in the distance, and I thought, *This is a peaceful place to die.* Since that day, I slowly learned a lesson that I had been avoiding for years, an avoidance that had fueled my frantic search for a home while simultaneously making it impossible to find. I finally began to pick up pieces of wisdom that I had been walking past for most of my life.

In Frances Sherwood's novel *Vindication,* a fictionalized account of the life of Mary Wollstonecraft, the tormented and occasionally suicidal protagonist is desperate to discover the right way to live. She tells her longtime friend and publisher that she is overwhelmed by "all that might be, not be, so be it, your mind going a hundred thoughts between this moment and the next." Her friend replies: "But my dear, you have arrived. You are here, at your life. Put yourself down, settle in. It is yours. You have been living it all along."

Years ago I was walking down a sun-washed street in Antigua, Guatemala. Kids rocketed by on little pipe-cleaner bikes. Nobody drinking coffee at the outdoor cafés reacted when the active volcano in the distance let out a soft puff at irregular intervals, as if it were taking slow, shallow breaths.

Passing an open doorway I saw a man teaching a woman to dance in a small, plain room. He watched her face as she counted softly to herself in English and dust spun in the sunlight on the floor around their moving feet. As I approached the end of the street, I watched a woman wearing a ragged backpack and long braids cross the cobblestones and knock on the door. She looked weary but eager. After waiting for a moment she knocked on the door again. I stopped and waited, too. Suddenly the door opened and a woman with long dark hair flung herself into the backpacker's arms. They pulled apart and looked at each other, hugged again. The two friends or lovers or sisters rocked from side to side, mouths trembling, one woman's arms barely able to reach around the other's huge pack, reunited. I felt homesick suddenly, for my friends, for connection. I could see so many of them in that moment. I bought a stack of postcards and scribbled a bunch of little love notes as the volcano belched softly in the distance. *I'm here in this place but do you remember when . . . xoxoxoxoxo.*

I, too, finally arrived. I got the transformation I longed for, but it didn't happen in the way I'd expected. I felt weirdly at home in my world in Santa Fe under a big sky with my beautiful, dying child. Walking on the arroyo path, listening to Ronan laugh, watching him eat and sleep and play, sitting with him on the couch, sometimes for hours, teaching my classes and writing my books. It was not the life I imagined, not the dollhouse, but it was home. In the midst of grief I often felt the way you do in that moment when you hold in your arms the person who has traveled a long way, maybe all their lives, to reach you.

4

Human beings have always been
mythmakers. The most powerful myths are
about extremity; they force us to go beyond
our experience. There are moments when
we all, in one way or another, have to go to
a place that we have never seen, and do what
we have never done before. Myth is about
the unknown; it is about that for which we
initially have no words. Myth therefore
looks into the heart of a great silence.

—Karen Armstrong, *A Short History of Myth*

Opening my eyes on that January morning after Ronan's
diagnosis was like waking up in an alternative universe—
a silent world, mindless and still and as bleak and vast as the
desert I lived in. Rick and I began the day with Ronan snuggled
in the bed between us. We cried. First Rick, then me, then Rick

again, then me again. We didn't know what to do, how to be with each other, with ourselves; we couldn't think of a thing to say. Terra incognita. We were bereft, quaking with a wild and terrible vibrancy. We had no narrative anchor, no arrow to point us in any direction that didn't promise misery as its endpoint. We were like Paleolithic people gazing into the sky with fearful awe and wondering what disaster or wonder would pour out of it next. The historian Rudolf Otto quoted by Karen Armstrong: *mysterium tremendum terribile et fascinans.* That was the first few days.

Then we began feeling around the future, lifting its edges, sniffing it out. We talked about taking Ronan for hikes again when the snow melted from the hiking trails near our house. We did a crossword puzzle but weren't able to fill in all the blanks. I forced myself to eat, and I forced myself to go out and get some exercise, even though there was a knot in my stomach that refused to loosen, and even though I felt a great need to escape the house and my life (and then felt guilty about this desire) and even though being out in the world felt like being flogged. Every image and sensation felt thunderous and unsafe. Kids and babies everywhere; preschools and grade schools and parks with jungle gyms; buggies and baby stores and pro-life billboards. I had to pull over three times in order to get it together enough to stay on the road. Certain places I affiliated with a nondiagnosed Ronan were suddenly off-limits, and I made a list: the Santa Fe Farmer's Market; certain coffee shops; the Antlers Hilton in Colorado Springs. It would be like walking around in the shadow of a former self holding the shadow of a former baby. I simply couldn't bear it.

When I saw my friend Carin at the gym, my best girlfriend since moving to Santa Fe, I told her about Ronan's diagnosis. I learned quickly how to tell people coldly, matter-of-factly and, of course, she was wonderful, offering love and support. We'd moved to Santa Fe in July 2010, but you would have thought we'd lived there for twenty years. Our friends Rob and Lala brought cinnamon buns and scones and jocular humor and kindness to our house. They bounced Ronan on their laps and warned us not to isolate. Nancy sent a huge basket of fancy deli food and researched elliptical trainers that we could buy for the back room so we could still get some exercise if we ended up staying home more. Terri and Jules helped Rick collect the machine in Terri's truck. All of this help was offered by people I didn't know well (yet) at all. I was grateful.

But when I told people what was happening in our little world on Sol y Luz Street, I felt a great divide—between me and other people, and also within me. As I said *my baby is dying* (from the very beginning I refused to sugarcoat), as those words left my mouth, I was conscious of the fact that there was a "me/mother" before I knew Ronan was sick and a "me/mother" now anticipating his death, and that these two people didn't know each other at all, and so I no longer understood how to relate to the person standing before me, waiting and wanting to help, even if it was someone I respected or even adored. With Rick, too, I felt as if I were shouting through a tidal wave of water and fire to connect with him, or trying to have a conversation in the middle of a tornado. *You have to stick together,* our friends and family told us. How, when we could hardly hear each other? All day my jaw hurt as if I'd been chewing the air.

When I got home from the gym, Ronan was sitting on my dad's lap, perfectly content. Rick was in the kitchen, where he'd begun to retreat on a daily basis, whipping up elaborate vegan meals, in order (I think) to have something to do with his hands. Chores were getting done at lightning speed. There wouldn't be one tissue in a wastebasket before he'd be dumping it out. "What are you doing?" I'd ask after a Xanax-induced nap. "Organizing the forks," he'd reply. Now he tossed onions into the skillet and I wandered into the bedroom, anxious to set my mind on something, anything, else.

I tried reading one of Rick's fantasy novels. Nope. I tried my usual go-tos: McCullers, Ondaatje, even Tolstoy failed me. I browsed through my small selection of fluffy, tra-la-la books. All narratives felt inane and pointless, even those with the obvious goal of being both.

I felt guilty reading at all, in fact, knowing that Ronan never would, that he would never understand stories, or at least not in the way that writers like me struggled and strained to make them known. And then I fell upon *Myths from Mesopotamia* sitting on top of the stack of books by my bed, a book I'd been reading in preparation to teach a Bible as Literature class. Stories that nobody could agree on! Perfect.

I cracked open the book and found precisely what I was looking for: big, bad distraction in the form of ancient myth. Royal epics translated from Akkadian! Accounts of historical kings from the second millennium BCE! Good old Gilgamesh in his fugue of grief after the loss of his dearest friend, his epic quest for immortality! Baal and his nasty nostrils! Never before—even while I was in divinity school—had I been so interested in the literary history of Babylonia and Assyria, these tales and fables that were precursors to many of the stories in the Bible.

Akkadian myths and epics and tales got shorter as they aged, not more elaborate. Later scribes simply included signposts, like an outline, for the teller, who was forced or, I guess, invited, often in the spirit of competition, to embellish the text with his or her own asides and ideas and performative techniques. The stories were cyclical and elliptical. Bony. The vocabulary in these later stories was crappy, the storytelling was sloppy, and the plots were ridiculous, at least in written form. The teller was left to fill in the blanks.

The people of Mesopotamia, a land between the Euphrates and Tigris rivers in modern Iraq, made myths and stories, they told tales and fables—as we all do—in order to understand who they were, who made them, what their purpose on the earth might be, and where they went when they died. And then there were those gaps. In some cases they intentionally left their history full of holes, in others the tablets were irrevocably damaged by time. Who knows what's missing? How did the story end? What was it like? The answers were forever lost thousands of years ago, and they will remain lost.

These earliest stories were written out of the primal human impulse to make meaning from chaos. Ronan's world, in some sense, would always be chaos, his brain unformed, his experience unordered. It would always be, as the late poet Jane Kenyon might say, "otherwise."

Was Ronan unhappy? No. He had no label for that.

Are we any happier when we know (or think we know) the difference between unhappy and happy? I doubt it. Life is really lived within those parentheticals, in what we don't know or expect, in what has already disappeared, in what is already gone. When Ronan's sensory faculties disappeared, did that mean that his narrative went with it, or did he simply exist in that gap, a place we could not access without relinquishing the desire to understand its parameters, to make sense of it?

The next day, brimming with myth, I drove past a Subaru with a tree strapped to the top—a new, healthy-looking, bushy-branched tree, not a tired old tree on its way to the dump during those first few weeks of January. Hm . . . maybe a family that decided to celebrate Christmas at the beginning of the year instead of at the end? Why would they do that? Who were these people? What color was the carpet in their living room? What did the husband and wife talk about when they went to bed at night? Did they still love each other? Already, I was telling a story. Trying to make meaning from a single moment. Why couldn't it just be a damn tree?

For Ronan, it could be. That was the secret of unlocking his myth; that was the way to read it, the guide. He lived and always would live in those gaps of knowledge, those careful, fragile holes in the script of story and meaning. We get angry and our skin gets warm. We get sad and we feel as if we've eaten a brick. And then we start ordering, and shaping, and sifting stories. We have our clay (the senses) and then we start throwing it around. We start messing with our tablets. We mistakenly think they'll last forever. (In the most moving section of his biography of Flannery O'Connor, Brad Gooch tells us that in her final moments, O'Connor was editing her stories, even hiding them under her hospital bed so that the nurses wouldn't see them and try to stop her.) For Ronan, there was no narrative process, there was only . . . what?

My mind wanted to make sense of Ronan's world, his experience, as if this would somehow make sense of why or how this could have happened to him and to me, as if I might, in theology or art or ancient myth, find some reason, some answer, some precedent. I wanted to be present for my son, but my mind needed to spin and spin and spin, searching for solutions, the salve of meaning, story, language. Instead I only generated more questions, a kind of frantic curiosity that would, for a brief moment, stave off the feelings of helplessness and rage, the gripping, shattering, closing-in sadness like two hands rattling the heart. I took Xanax, and I thought of taking more Xanax, the whole bottle, just to escape. I drank one glass of wine and then another. Everything in me wanted to look away, to disappear, and, often, to die. I called other moms and they talked me down, back into the room, back into the body, into my family, back to my baby. *He's not in pain. He doesn't know he's dying. It's hell, but you'll get through it; you'll survive.* And this, of course: *He needs you. You are his mother. This is your task, hellish as it might be. You have no choice.*

My other task beyond physical care, I began to realize, was to find Ronan's quiet, gap-ridden myth, his idiosyncratic narrative—to interpret it, share it, and learn from it. Mythology was the only solution, with its ability to, as Armstrong notes, "awaken us to rapture, even in the face of death and the despair we may feel at the prospect of annihilation . . . Like a novel, an opera or a ballet, myth is make-believe, it is a game that transfigures our fragmented, tragic world, and helps us to glimpse new possibilities by asking 'What if?'" Impossibly scary "what ifs" held within them some possibility, some opportunity to see the world in a different, more complex way. To dwell more consciously in the gray areas.

What if Ronan "described" his experiences to me? Would a touch be feathery? No, he had no concept of a feather. Words and descriptions were meaningless abstractions. He was simply going forward every moment and leaving everything behind. No analysis, no memory, no stress, no desire. He let everything pass; he let it all get lost. In that gap where he existed there was no map for his meaning. *But there will be,* I thought. If Ronan needed a myth, I would write one. If the only way to stop being divided from him, if the only way to dwell in his space, even for a moment, which I ardently, desperately wanted to do, was to stare into that silent world and make it speak, then I had work to do. I shut the book of ancient myths and returned to the living room to be with my family. Ronan was laughing in my mom's arms as she jumped across the room, pretending to be a bunny. "Here he is," my mom said, and flew him, Superbaby style, into my arms.

timeless
presence

5

January felt endless, lifted from a Victorian novel: I was hysterical, inconsolable, stricken. I had the urge to run down the street in pajamas (for lack of a period nightgown) tearing at my hair and wailing. Sometimes I was afraid to leave the house and would cower with Ronan in a corner like some crazy mama bear, as if Tay-Sachs were a predator or an intruder from whom I might protect him. I did, on some days, feel like Gilgamesh, the grieving man "howling bitterly" who cannot accept his grief at the loss of his beloved friend. He laments and paces; "he tears and messes his rolls of hair." He begs to be listened to: "Listen to me, Elders. Hear me out, *me* . . . An evil has risen up and robbed me." On other days, I felt unaccountably, almost brutally, happy, as if existence had been pared down to singular moments between Ronan and me. I was living in this state, I think, of death-meets-life, buoyed by the knowledge of an abyss that was empty without being hopeless. Vaclav Havel described the unexpected and euphoric happiness he experienced in prison like this:

> One is exhilarated, one has everything imaginable, one neither needs nor wants anything any longer—and yet simultaneously, it seems as though one had nothing, that one's happiness were no more than a tragic mirage, with no purpose and leading nowhere. In short, the more wonderful the moment, the more clearly that telltale question arises: and then what? What more? What else? What next? What is to be done with it and what will come of it? It is . . . an experience of the finite . . . a glimpse into the abyss of the infinite, of uncertainty, of mystery. There is simply nowhere else to go—except into emptiness, into the abyss itself.

The abyss, yes. (I remembered that line from a Jane Kenyon poem about the death of her father: "That's why babies howl; *this* is the abyss.") But our family still had details to sort out. Eventually we started to think, strategize and adjust. Instead of investigating future day care and preschool options, Rick and I drove to Albuquerque for appointments with neurologists and geneticists, all of whom told us that there was nothing they could do to save our son and very little they could do to ease his suffering. This was not easy for doctors to say, as the medical establishment is geared toward protecting the future.

For doctors, saving lives means extending lives. That's their job. By contrast, on that same day when we met with a pediatric hospice care team, the conversation was about quality of life, not quantity. There were dreadful, odious, unimaginable decisions to be discussed, to be made. Which seizure medications might be effective, and in what combinations? When Ronan could no longer swallow, would we decide to place a feeding tube no matter how his other faculties had been affected, or would we let nature take its course? At each stage of potential intervention, hospice care asks: "What does it lead to? What is it for?" Would we know how to listen to what Ronan's body was telling us? Or would we just desperately cling to our son?

I talked more with other moms of Tay-Sachs children, cobbling together a tentative care plan for Ronan and discussing avenues for advocacy, research and support for families. These mighty, indefatigable dragon moms gave me all the grim details, compassionately but matter-of-factly, and without hesitation or pity. "Things have a habit of changing around their birthdays," they warned. The traditional milestones turned on their heads. We no longer wondered "What if he starts talking today?" but "What if he stops smiling, cooing?" We didn't ask "I wonder when he'll take his first step," but "I wonder when he'll stop moving completely." A daily list of tyrannical what-ifs. What was supposed to mean one thing suddenly meant something else entirely. Waiting for change felt like waiting to be punched in the face, kicked in the gut, stretched out on some rusty medieval rack to be tortured slowly.

An elaborate taxonomy of transformation exists in our culture. Change your body, change your life, take charge of your financial future, stop wrinkles. Americans are driven by future-directed resolutions. We thrive on the idea of change, the business of ambition. My own childhood fantasy of transformation was just a more extreme variation on this theme. But Ronan would never speak, or write, or do much with his hands besides spin the little lizard inside the plastic egg on his bouncer, turn the pages of a soft book and bat the chimes of his dragon toy. He had, literally, no future. How did we understand the meaning and purpose of Ronan's life in a society—like most societies—that was dedicated to progress and achievement, where going back was synonymous with failure? Where the longer life was seen as the more successful one, the one worth fighting for? If you were unable to tell your own story, did it mean you didn't have one to tell?

We needed new words and a new language, and it could be created only through discourse, which could only happen between people using language to make their experiences known. Enter art in its purest form: mucking up meaning. Disrupting our worldview. Redescribing story, Ronan's story—his path, his myth—could blaze new pathways of understanding not only for me but for others.

As a young teenager in the late 1980s I was a counselor at an Easter Seals camp in Colorado. I remember so well watching one of the campers—she was about ten or eleven—sit up on a horse for the first time. I can't remember her specific disability, although I think it was spina bifida, but I do remember there were supports on the horse's saddle, and that she was so excited that she had been unable to eat breakfast. When she was finally situated, the horse trainer and I stepped away. She didn't move. She stared into the distance, completely still.

"You can tell her to go and she will, or I can nudge her," said the trainer, making a move toward the horse.

"No!" the girl shouted. "Don't!" The horse neighed and stomped a hoof lightly but stayed where she was. "I want to stay just like this. I want to be this. I want to be right here. *I am the horse.*" We looked at her. "I'll move when I want to," she told us.

And so she sat. For about twenty minutes. Each kid was only allotted thirty minutes, and I was getting worried that she'd regret not having gone somewhere, but she looked so peaceful that I didn't want to push her. We'd also had a bit of a wrangle getting ready that morning and she was still grumpy with me, so I was afraid that if I suggested a particular course of action, she would choose the opposite. I stayed quiet. Eventually she did take the horse on a slow trot around the corral, just one loop, and she was perfectly happy. She refused to let anyone else make that leap from experience to meaning on her behalf, and she was absolutely right to be suspicious of our motives. As I rocked Ronan to sleep that night, I thanked her for reminding me, years later, that new, authentic narratives, real stories, were possible to create, to recognize, and finally, to share.

6

How can I describe my emotions at this catastrophe, or how delineate the wretch whom with such infinite pains and care I had endeavored to form? The different accidents of life are not so changeable as the feelings of human nature. I had worked hard for nearly two years, for the sole purpose of infusing life into an inanimate object. For this I had deprived myself of rest and health. I had desired with an ardour that far exceeded moderation; but now that I had finished, the beauty of my dream vanished, and breathless horror and disgust filled my heart. Unable to endure the aspect of the being I had created, I rushed out of the room.

—Mary Shelley, *Frankenstein*

Ronan and I began the first day in February watching the room fill with light as snow crystals melted against the living room window. The blue spruce in front of the house across the street was slowly covered in white, as if it were aging as we stood there. I thought, *Ronan will never be an old man. Next month he'll be one year old, and then he might be two, but will he ever be three?* I tried to imagine Ronan as an old man, sitting in a recliner, a cup of tea in a saucer on a small table, snoozing in front of a Red Sox game, retired and worn out, his life a road he had run well, stretching out full and dark behind him. The image made me want to weep. *What if he had lived to a ripe old age and then gotten some terrible cancer?* I thought in a surreal, hopeful way. In the entire United States, only a dozen or so babies are diagnosed with Tay-Sachs each year. If Ronan would have eventually died of some rare and painful cancer, then maybe Tay-Sachs was a merciful way to go, because he didn't know what was happening to him and therefore he could not be afraid. This was clearly the logic of the desperate and the bereaved. "Gee," Ronan said, his single word. I put him in his bouncer. He batted at the blue frog on one side and then took aim at the red bird on the other, like a boxer hitting a slow bag instead of a speed bag, like a mellow DJ spinning tunes. His bouncing was already growing less vigorous, and we needed to pad the front and sides of the seat to keep him from pitching forward. A few months later, the bouncer disappeared, replaced with the swing he used to sleep in as a newborn.

I graded papers as Ronan bounced in slow motion and then I asked him, "Are you ready to start your baby day?" He was; there were textured pillows to touch and hair to pull; there were cloth books to drool on and yoga poses to be done (happy baby). I lifted him from the bouncer and sat him on my stomach. He laughed and lunged at my face. Noses were a particular favorite, although the holes in ears were also appreciated, and lips were an endless source of amusement. Fingers? Amazing. For one long moment he soberly studied me—he was always a philosophical dude—before breaking into a wide, wet smile that was more like a silent laugh. He would have been a great silent film star.

How long will Ronan be able to do happy baby? I wondered as he struck his pose on the changing table. In less than a year, Ronan would be blind. I could hardly imagine it—the light going out of his eyes but his heart beating on. He would have started having seizures that required medication. That, too, filled me with panic and dread. These images, and many others, kept jutting into my mind, toppling me, together with these lines from Gerard Manley Hopkins's poem about grief: *O the mind, mind has mountains; cliffs of fall / frightful, sheer, no-man-fathomed.*

In the days following his diagnosis ("Babies with Tay-Sachs can live three years with good care," I kept hearing the doctor intone), I was afraid to be alone with Ronan, terrified of the sadness and helplessness, the anger and fear that touching his head or his hands or his face provoked in me, these jagged feelings that punctured my day and made it difficult to do activities as simple as boiling water for tea, or pulling a few squares of toilet paper off the roll, thinking *Ronan will never be able to do anything as basic as this.* But on that first February morning, after his nap, I held Ronan without crying and waltzed him around the room without catapulting into the future. In an illogical way, this felt like progress.

Meanwhile, we were growing into Ronan's terminal diagnosis and its attendant jargon. "Will you insert a *feeding tube* when he can no longer eat?" "What are your plans for his *end-of-life* care?" "Are you open to interventions like a *chest vest* or a *suction machine* to assist with *secretion control* when Ronan can no longer manage on his own?" Rick and I knew that how we responded to these monstrous, seemingly impossible but necessary questions would determine not only the course but the end of our son's life. We sat stone-faced in the pediatrician's office, understanding that we would never be the same. We felt grotesque and out of place in our own lives. You can, for just a moment, fuse grief like a bone, but the memory of the ability to bend lingers inside, like an itch running in the blood, just beneath the skin: relief is always only temporary. Grief, we understood, would now hijack a part of our day for the rest of our lives, sneaking in, making the world momentarily stop, every day, forever.

And I kept remembering moments from my pregnancy. In November 2010 I was at Yaddo, an artist's colony in upstate New York, feverishly trying to finish the draft of a novel before Ronan was born. I was frantic, believing everybody's warnings that "you'll never have time to do anything once you have kids." (This turned out, of course, to be absolutely false and just another silly thing people say, such as "Enjoy it now!" or "It's only downhill from here" when one is pregnant and buying groceries at the store, filling the car with gas, et cetera.) I went a little feral during that time, typing away in my writing room—a sun porch clearly better suited for summer residents, with three walls made entirely of floor-to-ceiling windows. Until I finally admitted that the austerity of the cold was not assisting my creative process and decided to ask for a space heater from the kind caretaker who resembled Walt Whitman, I wore long underwear beneath corduroys and an oversized wool sweater, my heavy down coat and pink fingerless gloves (perfect to type in!) knitted by my friend Tara.

One morning, just before dawn, when I hadn't spoken to another person in nearly three days, hadn't eaten a single meal that did not involve peanut butter, and hadn't slept more than two hours a night in nearly a week but instead had restless, almost violent naps full of vivid and labyrinthine dreams, I felt my stomach muscles begin to shake and then *move apart*. My ribs started to ache; when I touched them they were electric, ropy wires of vibrating bone, and they, too, were on the move. Muscles cracking, bones stretching. Ronan. The two of us were alone in that room; you probably could have seen the lights in our windows from a long way off.

A few skinny deer nosed around in the scattering of snow outside my window, unimpressed with my artistic ambitions. The trees were cocooned in ice. A terrified-looking squirrel slid ungracefully down a glassy branch and then scurried out of sight. I could see lights on in the house across the road; other early risers or still-awake night owls were up and writing. Ronan kept kicking and elbowing and I felt my stomach swell beneath my palms. Ronan making himself known, taking up a bit more space, stretching out the tight trampoline of my midsection. *Here I am.* I remember saying out loud, "I see you." And later, I did. Checking my e-mail before dinner, I saw that Rick had sent me the digital photograph of our 3-D ultrasound results. I took a breath before I opened the file. There he was, our little Zoat, as we had already nicknamed him, with a face that looked as if it were still being molded and shaped, a baby in process, claylike and soft and sepia-toned. He looked, frankly, like a slightly misshapen cat in midmeow. But there was a clear nose, eyes that looked squeezed shut, the thin angle of a hand near his mouth. I looked down at my stomach. How had the clay changed from that image to this moment? Had those little webby hands I saw on the screen been pushing at my rib cage? What new part had been stitched together? Another resident was sitting next to me when I gasped and said, "Look! That's my son! He looks like a malformed cat! Isn't he cute?" She craned her neck to get a view of my screen. "Wow," she said, and put a hand on my shoulder. "Thanks for showing me this. I'll never forget it." *Me, neither,* I thought. I could hardly believe he was mine.

At Yaddo I reread Mary Shelley's *Frankenstein,* one of the only books on the communal shelves that interested me. Sitting in my cold glass room I found it just as creepy and disturbing and wonderfully melodramatic as I had almost two decades before.

Some speculation surrounds the origin of Shelley's idea for her story of a "modern Prometheus." She was obviously familiar with the Greek myth, and the book's epigraph is from *Paradise Lost,* but I like to imagine that the initial creative spark was a bit more complicated. Mary Shelley's mother, Mary Wollstonecraft, author of the hugely influential early feminist text *A Vindication of the Rights of Woman,* died giving birth to her daughter. That itself is a kind of ghost story, a nightmare tale. And Mary Shelley would not be immune to her own private horrors surrounding creation.

While summering in Geneva, Mary and her friends experienced a weird burst of freakishly cold and nasty weather. As legend has it, in order to pass the time (no *Real Housewives of Zurich* or *French Riviera Shore* for these astute literary minds; they had to make do with imagination!), they sat inside around the fire and read one another German ghost stories, and then they each agreed to write their own story. Mary, eighteen years old, was the only one who finished hers. It was published anonymously the following year, in 1818.

I imagined Mary (Mary Godwin at the time) chilling out by the fire with her lover, Percy Shelley, Lord Byron and his pregnant lover, Claire, in odd summer weather described politely in some accounts as "ungenial." The seasons have gotten confused, and this brainy group is fascinated with current scientific attempts to "animate" dead matter—a movement called, appropriately, "galvanism"—and from this convergence of factors the urge to write ghost stories springs. In later accounts of the origin of her story, Mary claimed to have written *Frankenstein* in a "waking dream." I had plenty of those at Yaddo. Dreams in which falling rain became thick ropes of hair, then rubber, then iron bars.

Dr. Frankenstein, too, creates at a feverish clip, although he knew very little about what he was doing—with the brain, with the body, with the changes of his own heart and mind after he created his being, although at the beginning of the book he feels like a master of the universe, the smartest man in any room. Frankenstein is strenuously ambitious, obsessed with science and creating "natural wonder." He beavers away at his creation, literally stitching him together (and here Mary *must* have been thinking of the psalmist who thanks God for being "fearfully and wonderfully made"). But instead, the monster looks funny. This experimentation with "the unhallowed arts" did not work out the way he'd planned. The monster is not baby cute. He has yellow skin and bulging veins and is twice the size of a normal man. Frankenstein flees from him, frightened and horrified.

The rest of the book is a dramatic caper complete with Dickensian moments of coincidence in the plot, with the creator actively seeking to destroy his creation and vice versa. An innocent child is murdered and the wrong person is blamed. Frankenstein falls sick, is nursed back to health, and is eventually imprisoned, picking up a long-suffering wife along the way. He stumbles into much of this trouble in part because he refuses to listen to his creation, who is pursuing him—initially, at least—with a single, relatively simple goal: to be loved and acknowledged. The monster, who is never given a name but is identified in the text as "wench" or "it" or other equally pleasant monikers, learns about human love by sitting in the woods, literally set apart, watching a human family giving and receiving tenderness, experiencing grief and anger and joy and forgiveness, moving through various stages of life and relationship. When he finally reaches out to them in the spirit of human connection, he is violently and mercilessly rejected. Hurt, alone and super pissed off, he heads out with a new mission: to find his creator and then kick his ass for abandoning him in a world where he finds only rejection.

I had a complicated relationship with the book when I first read it in junior high school English class. I identified with the characters and the emotions in the book, but I was also deeply uncomfortable that I identified more closely with the monster than with Frankenstein. I was the new kid in a new school in a new state. Each month we drove six hours to another state, where I had adjustments made to a wooden leg, a clunky contraption that leaked and creaked and gave me disgusting sores that were sometimes so painful that I had to grit my teeth when I walked to and from my locker between classes. I was poked and prodded by a creepy prosthetist whose skin reminded me of a wax statue, and then in the hospital I was X-rayed and examined and sized up. The process felt monstrous and made me feel freaky. (Going through TSA checks each time I fly is not a dissimilar experience.)

We also happened to be reading *Frankenstein* during the basketball section of gym class. I could not run then, but I had to take gym in order to graduate, so the teacher devised a brilliant solution: at the end of every session, I would be called onto the court, where I would stand in the free throw lane, a little bit unstable—my artificial feet were literally foam blocks then—as the rest of the class threw balls to me, one by one, and collectively counted how many I could then sink. I spent thirty minutes sitting on the bleachers, shivering with anticipation as I prepared for this task, trying to imagine myself out on the court, nailing twenty perfect free throws: *swish, swish, swish.* As it turned out, I did sink a lot of those balls. In the late 1950s my dad was a high school all-star player at his high school in rural Illinois and he often shot hoops with me in the driveway of our house. My mom won the free throw competition at her fiftieth high school reunion, which was also my father's. I always was a good shot. But the anxiety of this experience—of being different, set apart—has never fully left me.

In junior high I empathized with Dr. Frankenstein as well.

All that work, and then *poof!* A monster in the house! Not a cuddly baby, not a child prodigy, not even a proper man. A menace, a fiend, a wretch, a freak. Who would want to be blamed for creating a monster that lives to wreak such havoc? Reconsidering the book in the context of Ronan's life, I wanted to tell Dr. F to man up and stop being such an asshole. Be a father already, because that's what you are. You created this being who was waiting and worthy of your love, and actually a pretty nice guy until you treated him badly, and then you abandoned him because you were scared and unprepared for the randomness and chance that is a part of every creative act, and because his future was dangerous and unpredictable, and because he wasn't a small, delicate-fingered, to-the-manor-born scientist with a fancy Swiss pedigree, and because people were no doubt going to look at him and judge him and then judge you. Get over it. Havoc happens on its own, with or without your clever machinations. Stand by your man, you cowardly ninny, even if he has greasy yellow skin and a big head and has to crouch down when he walks through doorways. Understand that when you die, it will be the man you made and tried to destroy who weeps over your grave, his wish granted but his heart broken. *Oh, Frankenstein! Generous and self-devoted being! What does it avail that I now ask thee to pardon me? I, who irretrievably destroyed thee by destroying all thou lovedst? Alas! He is cold; he may not answer me.*

7

I held tight
Thinking
What the hands lose
Is for the eyes to find
And what the eyes lose
Is for the heart to find
But the heart
When it loses a thing
Is left to fend for itself.

—Philip Pardi, "Two Hands"

Ronan and I took a lot of walks in February, his little face pressed to my chest, his body snuggled up to mine in his front pack, his gurgling voice ringing out into the cold, still air. Several people expressed to me that because all parents want their children to be perfect, they had trouble imagining my feelings about Ronan's condition, and, I guess, about Ronan.

They wondered why Rick and I hadn't both been tested for the Tay-Sachs gene, as if we'd given no thought at all to starting a family, or they tell their own stories about being nervous about Tay-Sachs and then feeling so relieved when their children turned out to be just fine, that they weren't like Ronan, that they didn't have to live our life. The comments in missives tinged with pity and selfishness made me livid, and seemed more about the senders than about Ronan. They were useful to nobody in the absence of compassion, which was always in short supply and needed by everyone. These things were said, no doubt, in a spirit of support, and I understood that people struggled for the right words with which to respond to people's difficult or "abnormal" situations. I'd been rattling off my life story to strangers in elevators for years when asked, "Oh my. What's wrong with you?" I would respond with a quick story about me, my artificial leg, how it happened, et cetera. "Oh, uh, I'm so sorry." (If there were a single phrase I could choose never to hear again in my life, it would be "I'm sorry.")

Mary Shelley heard "I'm sorry" often, no doubt, from her married lover and from friends and family who helped her bury her dead children. Imagine the response to this letter from Hogg, a friend she wrote to after the death of her first child, a premature daughter:

My dearest Hogg my baby is dead—will you come to see me as soon as you can. I wish to see you—It was perfectly well when I went to bed—I awoke in the night to give it suck it appeared to be sleeping so quietly that I would not awake it. It was dead then, but we did not find that out till morning—from its appearance it evidently died of convulsions—Will you come—you are so calm a creature & Shelley is afraid of a fever from the milk—for I am no longer a mother now.

A woman, a writer, a creator speaking here from inside a tunnel of grief, a tunnel that in those dark days of winter I was slowly learning to navigate, learning its exact size and shape and levels of darkness and how these shifted from moment to moment. I wanted to go back in time and appear as a ghost who miraculously lights a candle in the middle of the night at Mary's bedside, or show up in one of her waking dreams bearing a magic wand, like that luminous fairy queen in *The Lord of the Rings* who gives Frodo a special little stick to use "when all other lights have gone out." Or maybe I'd just play John Lennon's "Imagine" on a constant loop from an invisible sound system, the song that was playing as I sat writing by my own fire in those early months of 2011, knowing that someday I would be sitting by the same fire but I would not be the same person, and I would no longer be a mother.

It was difficult—maybe even impossible—for me to imagine that Ronan was not, in his own way, perfect, if only because he was living the only way he could. There was a great deal of perfection—and rare innocence—in that. He would never look like the other kids; he would be alone at the free throw lane in almost every respect. "I don't want to take him to the children's play area while I do yoga because he can't *play*," Rick said to me one afternoon, his voice cracking. "What if he just sits in the corner by himself? If he falls over he can't push himself back up." Neither one of us could stand the thought. There were so many things from which I had no way of protecting my child, thoughts that put me right at the thinning edge of sanity. But one thing I knew: Ronan would not, like Frankenstein's monster, be sitting out in the middle of a dark forest, lonely, perched on a log and wishing somebody loved him. Not my boy.

Ronan was mine. Mine and Rick's. Of course we would have done anything to help him, to save him, but we didn't want him to be another, different baby. We couldn't imagine not having had a part in creating him, or not having known him, or loved him so fiercely. We weren't running away from him or rushing out of any rooms. We stayed put. And we never wanted him to be perfect. We wanted him to *live*.

I'd never experience with Ronan so much of what I'd been looking forward to as a mom: marveling as he acquired language, teaching him to ski, traveling with him to all of the wonderful places I have lived, helping him learn how to be a unique person in this mad world. He missed all his milestones on the pediatrician's developmental chart; there were no more boxes to tick or leave blank. I was angry about the unfairness of that, but I also knew this: he would never experience shame, regret, fear, self-loathing, worry, anxiety, or stress—all products of an ambitious search for happiness or recognition or whatever else we think will save us, things Dr. Frankenstein thought would save him and that led to his heartbreak and demise, things he thought would free him but only bound him more tightly. Ronan would never wish himself to be different. That state of existence was so far outside my own experience that I could scarcely imagine what it might be like. My terminally ill son was absolutely wondrous to me in this way, and there was no box to document this amazement, this respect, this difficult lesson.

Americans love the idea of "the pursuit of happiness." We love that this mandate is written into our fabric as a people. Ronan taught me that this myth has outlived its usefulness, if indeed it ever had any. Or else we've misread it, because this notion of ambition has been a problem, literally, for thousands of years.

In the Babylonian myth of Atrahasis, the earliest recorded version of the Flood story and a precursor to the biblical story of Noah and his famous ark, the gods get fed up with lifting stones and digging out rivers. They want rest. They demand that other creatures do some of the work so they can hang out and be immortal and engage in smiting and other violent and more entertaining pursuits. They stage a revolt, and it is eventually decided that new creatures—humans, made from blood and dirt—will be created to do the shitty, backbreaking stuff. And so the gods get their freedom and humans are left to try and break free of their circumstances, to change their lives.

Our country runs on the pursuit of achievement and ambition, and on the effects of individual striving. It's a capitalistic and therefore limited and problematic approach to vocation and purpose. For most of my life I was an ambition addict (be the thinnest, the smartest, the funniest, the *best*), and I found fuel for this addiction everywhere I looked. On bumper stickers ("My child is an honor student at—— School"); in the assumed joys of becoming an Avon saleswoman ("It's amazing what you can achieve with a bit of passion and hard work; call I-800-AVON!"); in the barrage of ads for diet products that always appear on January I ("5 weeks to a NEW YOU! Includes the cost of food!"). In I981, as the poster child for the Wyoming March of Dimes, I was quoted in the local newspaper as saying, "If you believe in yourself, you can do anything."

Do more, be skinnier, get richer, be famous (and then be even more famous), get a bigger house and a bigger car and a hotter girlfriend and a better life. *Be* better. When did having a good life mean living one that other people envied? Behind this drive to achieve lurks a deeper desire to be transformed. The standards for what is "normal" have become so formalized and yet so restrictive that people need a break from that horrible feeling of never being able to measure up to whatever it is they think will make them acceptable to other people and therefore to themselves. People get sick with this idea of change; I have been sick with it. We search for transformation in retreats, juice fasts, drugs and alcohol, obsessive exercise, extreme sports, sex. We are all trying to escape our existence, hoping that a better version of us is waiting just behind that promotion, that perfect relationship, that award or accolade, that musical performance, that dress size, that raucous night at a party, that hot night with a new lover. Everyone needs to be pursuing something, right? Otherwise, who are we? How about, quite simply, people? How about human? This is the great message of Shelley's *Frankenstein.* Part of Ronan's myth was this acknowledgment that we need the freedom to be people, that's all.

On Valentine's Day I dressed Ronan in his "All You Need Is Love" T-shirt with its black-and-white photograph of the Beatles. I took him to acupuncture with Dr. Janet. I fed him heaping spoonfuls of chocolate ice cream. I wondered what he would be like next year—what kind of medications he would be on, what kind of movement he would still be able to make, if he would be able to see me, if he would still be eating comfortably, if he would even be alive. What kind of baby would he be? The answer: mine. Even after he was dead: mine. Wasn't that enough?

Not for everyone. In the summer of 2002 I taught "gifted and talented kids" (I don't believe in that terminology, as it almost always means rich kids, nothing more) at Stanford for a summer session. The class was called "Writing and Imagination," and the kids were smart and funny and, of course, creative, although several of them did complain to me that they had gotten stuck in my boring writing class because their math scores weren't high enough. Most of them were also curiously stressed out. They would write a story or a poem and then nervously show me what they'd written, asking, "Did I do it right?" I tried to explain to them that creativity, by its very nature and definition, allows for variation; that there is no "right" way. They blinked at me and returned to their seats, often giving me the hairy eye because I'd refused to answer their question with a simple yes or no.

One girl, I'll call her Sananda, never asked me if her stories were "right" or "good." They were, in fact, extraordinary. She took risks in terms of image and metaphor and plot. Sometimes she added beautiful pencil illustrations in the margins. Our classrooms were often mysteriously without air-conditioning, and so we did a lot of our writing outside. Sananda liked to be apart from the others. I'd see her sitting in a patch of shade away from the group; writing, yes, but sometimes looking dreamily off into space. Once I watched her turn her hand over and over again in the stream of water from a fountain for almost five minutes. She smiled at me when she turned her stories in and then trotted off to the cafeteria, where every day, without fail, she ate French fries and a chocolate milkshake for lunch (ah, writers and their rituals). During mealtimes the other kids rattled off the different camps they were attending that summer: Shakespeare camp, drama camp, dude ranch camp, art camp. "That's a lot of camps," I said to one girl. "My parents like to get rid of me during the summer," she said matter-of-factly, and turned away to fill her glass with a weird mixture of Coke and Sprite. Sananda dipped her fries into her milkshake (two at a time, I noticed, always two) and stared out the window. I wondered why she was so different from the others.

And then I met the kids' parents. One mother demanded that her son put a quarter in a jar during mealtimes if he didn't use a new vocabulary word during conversation (apparently she kept an exhaustive list at the dinner table). A father asked me, "Approximately how long, in terms of hours, should it take him to complete a publishable short story?" My response— "Decades"—did not go over well. Another mother told me that even though her son wasn't as smart as his sister, she hoped that he could *at least* show some creative prowess; otherwise he'd never get into Harvard, and that would clearly be a disaster. The kids sat with their parents during these conversations and heard every critical word. I felt them shrinking before my eyes, and all my desperate heaps of praise in that moment would never compensate for the scathing critiques from the two people in the world who were supposed to love them absolutely, without conditions and without strings.

And then there was Sananda's mom. This was her question: "Is my daughter having fun? She looks so happy right now." I told her I thought Sananda *was* having fun ("I am!" Sananda agreed), and that she was also quite talented. "Well," said her mother, affectionately ruffling her daughter's hair, "of course she is. We just want her to explore and have a good time this summer. And she likes to tell stories and she loves to read." I was almost a decade away from being a mother, but I remember thinking that this mother's attitude about her daughter's particular gifts was a lesson in how to mother a child (and the way I had been mothered myself). I also worried that I would fail, that I would push my child too hard.

While my parents were still staying with us, Rick and I

went out for a Valentine's Day dinner, but it was hardly romantic. We struggled with what to say to each other. We were used to talking about the baby, planning for the future, looking forward, tracking change. Gone were our plans for Ronan's future. Gone was our hope. How could we talk about what was coming next—seizures, blindness, death—over samosas and vegetable biryani? We ate in silence and on the drive home I started to cry. The stars looked mean and bright and close in an unyielding winter sky. "It's as if there's another baby behind this baby, and we'll never get to meet him." Rick agreed this was unfair. I stopped crying and we rode home in silence. What about all the things I'd imagined that Ronan might be or become without Tay-Sachs in his way? We'd never know.

What I did know was that there would be no vocab jars for Ronan. There was nothing he needed to prove or do or become. He could stay a beautiful acorn; he didn't need to grow into a tree or realize his potential. He disproved Aristotle's teleological theory that potential is the key to life. No time limits for writing short stories or doing anything else. No pressure to be quicker or better or smarter than the other kids. If he wanted to roll over, great; when he could no longer do that, he could lie on his stomach and coo until that grew tiresome, and then we'd find another activity he enjoyed. He could eat avocados, touch the fabric of different pillows, my sweater, my hair (wet and dry), and read *Fishy Tales* (the best-selling book around here; it would easily win all the awards). He didn't have to meet any milestones. He could lie on his back and sit on our laps and do nothing at all. He didn't have to be self-reflective or worry about what was next or why life was the way it was or what his very short one was about or for. He would have his own way as a baby, his own set of "baby days." I tried to experience these with him—without judgment or expectation, understanding that being liberated is not the same as being free. I did not make Dr. Frankenstein's mistake and turn away.

Ronan saw no other baby waiting in the wings. No pursuit. No desire. There was only, simply, happiness. For him, yes, but the situation was, of course, more complicated for me, his mother. "The hardest part, my dear," my orthopedic surgeon wrote to me when I told him about Ronan's diagnosis, "is to reconcile your heart."

8

Affliction would not have this power
without the element of chance
contained by it.

—Simone Weil, *Waiting for God*

At the beginning of March I received a copy of my medical
records, faxed from Los Angeles, which included the entirety of my prenatal testing results. Looking at them, I felt
physically ill. A thick stack of blurry ultrasounds, check-up
sheets covered in acronyms, numbers divided by decimal points.
Comments about amniotic fluid and the baby's positioning,
weight gain and blood test results. Illegible doctor's notes. The
results of my Tay-Sachs carrier screening test? NO MUTA-
TION DETECTED. Standard prenatal screens detect only
nine common mutations of the gene, those most common
among the Ashkenazi Jewish population, but there are more
than one hundred mutations and counting (this is explained in

very small print beneath the results). Most kids with Tay-Sachs are now born to parents who didn't know they had anything to worry about. The gene, in other words, is everywhere. Why in this person or that person? Why in one and not the other? My superrare mutation, found, to my great surprise, among those of Moroccan descent, was hard to find—elusive, slippery, and all this time it had been lurking, waiting. Here, in Ronan, was the great unveiling of what, if odds had been in our favor, I would have never known.

I had the test, so I had done my part in preventing this. (Relief.) Many of my friends didn't even bother with prenatal testing—they simply trusted in the odds. Never having been one to believe that statistics were on my side (my own congenital birth defect is so very, very rare), I did everything to cover all the bases, get the results, to *know.* A genetic "test" now appeared to be about as foolproof as a weather prediction. (Rage.)

As soon as I learned I was pregnant I became obsessed with odds. I quickly ordered every prenatal test available to me, even those I was told, "based on my background," were unnecessary, including the test for Tay-Sachs. I cut out caffeine, alcohol, diet soda (chemicals!) and refined sugar. I drank buckets of water.

One of my favorite poets, who was probably not thinking about genetics in the strictest sense, though she was absolutely thinking about survival in which genes play a significant, unavoidable part, wrote one of my favorite poems about the paper-thin concept of luck and what if and how do you know and what might have happened and coulda shoulda woulda. I read it as a hard-edged take on the idea of being blessed, and survival of the fittest, and other things people believe in or say or misinterpret, phrases we live by, mistake, and perhaps—who knows?—grow to understand.

COULD HAVE

It could have happened.
It had to happen.
It happened earlier. Later.
Nearer. Farther off.
It happened, but not to you.
You were saved because you were the first.
You were saved because you were the last.
Alone. With others.
On the right. The left.
Because it was raining. Because of the shade.
Because the day was sunny.
You were in luck—there was a forest.
You were in luck—there were no trees.
You were in luck—a rake, a hook, a beam, a brake,
a jamb, a turn, a quarter inch, an instant.
You were in luck—just then a straw went floating by.
As a result, because, although, despite.

What would have happened if a hand, a foot,
within an inch, a hairsbreadth from
an unfortunate coincidence.
So you're here? Still dizzy from another dodge,
close shave, reprieve?
One hole in the net and you slipped through?
I couldn't be more shocked or speechless.
Listen,
how your heart pounds inside me.

—Wislawa Szymborska

Because, because. Why why why. The following week, after days of sunshine, we had day after day of snow—dry, chaotic flakes that fell in soft, twisting loops. The single plow in Santa Fe could not clear the roads and many of my classes were canceled. I was oddly disappointed. Going to work, having things to do, tasks, a show to run in the classroom was sometimes easier than staying at home. Even though I loved being with Ronan, it was also true that when I looked at him, I felt myself sliding into the place where crying would only dig a deeper, darker pit. Sometimes I would sit in my office after class and think *What if I just sat here for a moment and pretended to have a completely different life? What if I jumped out the window?* Everywhere I looked there were kids on sleds, kids peering out of windows with their chins propped in their hands, looking bored, kids bundled up and toddling with their parents through parking lots in bright jackets and playful hats, the sky white-gray and bottomless when it had once been a sparkling, peppy blue.

"He looks weaker," I told Rick the morning of the snowstorm. "Floppy."

"Really?" Rick took him from me and held him for a moment. "Hey, Zoat," he said. He propped him in the corner of the minicouch. Ronan toppled forward a bit, then to the side, but no more than usual. "He looks the same to me," Rick said, and picked him up again. My chest hurt, watching them. Part of the pain of Ronan's diagnosis was the fear of what it would do to Rick, who fathered him beautifully, attentively, lovingly. His parenting approach was patient, soft but intense, earnest and honest and, above all, vigilant. I wished I could spare Rick the pain of his son's loss. I wished I could spare myself.

Rick handed Ronan back to me, and as if to be sure that I knew he wasn't so floppy yet, Ronan kicked me, lifted his head and let out his version of a yell—a long coo moving into a high-pitched sigh. We'd been reading (cautiously, and in little bits at a time) about how Tay-Sachs progresses, how our world would gradually, slowly, inevitably change, but not as we had expected or hoped. Ronan had already stopped rolling over and could no longer control his head. At night when we put him in his crib we turned him gently on his stomach. He no longer did happy baby. When I changed his diaper, I lifted him into the pose, hoping it still made him feel good. I rocked his hips from side to side and massaged the bottoms of his feet. But he was beginning to belong more to the disease and less to us, it seemed, less to himself or what he might have been if his other genetic material had gotten a chance to manifest itself.

In her achingly beautiful book *The Member of the Wedding*, Carson McCullers, through the character of Frankie, exquisitely renders the feeling of separation from the world, and what it feels like to understand that there is an inevitable end to belonging:

> It was the year when Frankie thought about the world.
> And she did not see it as a round school globe, with the
> countries neat and different-colored. She thought of the
> world as huge and cracked and turning a thousand miles
> an hour.

Frankie understands that the world is grinding away from her every day. Moments are turning over, appearing and disappearing without her involvement or permission or knowledge, and they'll keep turning after she's gone. She is nothing but she is also everything, and this is so disorienting that she vacillates between never wanting to leave the hot and dirty little kitchen in her house and threatening to board a train and abandon her hometown for good. As the summer day cools into evening she sulks under trees and yells at her beloved cousin as she contemplates her limited options. She is itching to be out of her own skin; she can't live inside the feeling, this uncertainty that she cannot name. She wants to be a member of her brother's wedding, but she knows (and now she will never *not* know and it's maddening, maddening) that no relationship—with a sibling or a parent or a friend or a child, or in a body—lasts forever. As I read the book again (for the tenth time? the twentieth?), it was the first time I understood it as a stunning, quiet, almost perfect portrait of grief. Sometimes I tried to literally kick out of my grief, scratch my way out of it, rock away from it, scream it away, cry it out, and I understood why people cut themselves, how it was possible to want to die, to just end it, because none of my grieving strategies provided any relief. You end up where you started, running along a gravel road in the dark as dust obscures your vision and crowds your lungs. Who knew where you were headed? The year of Ronan's diagnosis was the year when I thought a lot about luck.

Although one of Ronan's genes was later identified as one of the nine mutations common among the Ashkenazi Jewish population (Rick's), after his DNA was sequenced, another very rare but identifiable gene was discovered—one associated with those of Moroccan heritage. I was expecting Irish, even Jewish. A part of my family is German, so the latter seemed possible, if unlikely, and would have been a great conversation starter (or stopper, in fact) at the next family reunion, and would also, I thought, speak to my desire to convert to Judaism four years earlier. French Canadian also seemed likely. But Moroccan? Really? My parents both grew up in a small town in central

Illinois. Farm country. German. Irish. Norwegians and Swedes. Protestants and Catholics and that's it. As children would they have been able to even find Morocco on a map?

Persecution and isolation gave rise to the Tay-Sachs gene: Eastern European shtetls isolated from the non-Jewish community, a separation enforced by pogroms and other forms of violence, forced people together and led to intermarriage, as did the colonial boot in Ireland and parts of the UK. The gene has been discovered among French Canadians and Cajuns, although it is still widely—and incorrectly—known as a "Jewish" disease. In fact, the Ashkenazi Jewish population has been so vigilant about testing that the number of affected babies in the Jewish community has declined greatly since the 1970s due to increased awareness and the fact that the standard prenatal test screens only for those mutations common among this particular population. "We really don't know who we are," the geneticist reminded me, "or how old these genes are, or where they come from." His voice, calm and reassuring, and then, in my head, the genetic counselor at Cedars-Sinai in Los Angeles, surprised that I'd had the Tay-Sachs test at all, saying "The odds are astronomical that you would be a carrier if you're not Jewish or of Eastern European descent." Enter Morocco. Or someone who went to Morocco, or someone kicked out of Spain who ended up in Morocco and then went to Switzerland or the Czech Republic or Germany or Ireland—all the places I'm "from," all these accidents of geography. Who are we? Where do we belong?

Nobody knows exactly where these genes are from or how old they are, and perhaps it wouldn't help to know, but I couldn't help wanting more information, and wishing, not for the first time in my life, that the word "rare" was not associated with any aspect of my physical body. I had red hair (rare), a disability (a rare one); before laser eye surgery I had severe myopia (also rare!); a valve in my heart did something funky with blood moving into a particular chamber that wasn't life threatening but was still rare (or at least relatively); and now I had a child with a terminal illness (again, rare, too rare). I wanted, just for a moment, to be normal. I wanted a rest-of-my-life break from being rare.

As a child I remembered seeing *When Bad Things Happen to Good People* by Harold Kushner on my parents' nightstand and being intrigued by the title, although I didn't read it until years later.

Kushner, a rabbi, tells the story of his child's death from a rare aging disease. Like Job, Kushner interrogates luck and God; he uses theology to try to understand why this situation has befallen *him*. He's a rabbi! He should have an in with God! He gets no answers, of course, but his book struck a powerful chord with millions of readers, if only because it admitted how deeply we are mystified by luck, even though we invoke the word frequently and often use it thoughtlessly. When I was born with a birth defect, a nurse said to my dad, a Lutheran pastor, "I can't believe this would happen to a man of God," as if he (a) deserved special treatment as a result of his vocation, or (b) his luck had run out. Both approaches are patently ridiculous, but it's incredible how these attitudes still permeate our thinking: we get upset when "good" people get cancer; we say someone is nice and isn't it unbelievable that he or she has had such crappy luck because he or she doesn't "deserve" it? Which begs the question: who deserves bad luck? Kushner:

> I don't think we should confront one another with our troubles. ("You think you've got problems? Let me tell you my problems, and you'll realize how well off you are.") That sort of competitiveness accomplishes nothing. It is as bad as the competitiveness that spawns sibling rivalry and jealousy in the first place . . . it would help if we remembered this: Anguish and heartbreak are not evenly distributed throughout the world, but they are distributed very widely. Everyone gets his share. If we knew the facts, we would very rarely find someone whose life was to be envied.

The flip side of this is what the thinker Simone Weil referred to as the dangers of a false sense of the heroic. Whenever someone experiences an event we might deem "unlucky" (like having a baby with a terminal illness), they often immediately flip into "you're so brave," which is a distancing maneuver disguised as a compliment. Behind these words you can practically here a voice screaming *Don't ever ever please please please don't let it happen to me; at least that didn't happen to me; so glad it's you not me; I hope my luck holds out (knock on wood).*

Luck. What is it? Who gets it and who doesn't and why? Is it contagious, like an STD, like a rash? Does bad luck beget bad luck like that weird "so-and-so begat so-and-so" list in the Bible, a portion of which I once memorized for an Old Testament/Hebrew Bible exam in divinity school? Can you get slotted into the lucky track and just stay put? "You're so lucky," we say to someone when something terrific happens to them: a new job, an award, a new lover, an engagement, a longed-for pregnancy. "You've had a streak of bad luck," we say to someone else who crashes their car three times in one month or gets dumped without explanation or gets sacked at work for no reason. Lucky. It's the title of a searing memoir by Alice Sebold. It's an overpriced clothing brand and a silly magazine devoted to the "art" of shopping. It's everywhere, and yet it's meaningless. Luck is a word (just a word) that we use to describe an event that's already happened. The word is wholly retrospective. We only know how it *did* go, not how it *might* have gone. The combinations of possible outcomes are truly endless. You can be virtuous and still get hit by a bus. If you're going to pursue virtue, it's best not to do so with the idea that it will cut you any breaks or grant you a free pass from cancer or divorce or natural disaster or heartbreak or any other potential loss.

We don't like this. We want will; we think relentless self-improvement will literally improve our lives, allow us to literally control our happiness; we want to believe we have power over our own destinies. We, quite simply, do not have any control, not really, and this is perhaps the hardest lesson to learn. After Ronan's diagnosis I often stood over him sleeping in his crib and wished I could lie next to him, press him to me, untangle his DNA, restitch it, rebraid it, fix it, make it right, take it back somehow, change the odds. (*How can there be mysteries this size?*—Naomi Shihab Nye, "Little Seal".) I marveled at how beautiful he was, how wonderfully made, and yet, from the moment of his birth (and even before), Tay-Sachs had been chipping away at him, unmaking him in some bizarre reversal, with each lived experience taking him backward into a world he (and I) would never fully know or understand. I hovered there, feeling like a just-picked scab, raw and messy and cold, remembering lines from "Settings," a favorite Seamus Heaney poem: *Where does spirit live? / Inside or outside / Things remembered, made things, unmade?* I swayed and grappled, thinking of walking with Ronan through the changing aspens of the Sangre de Cristo Mountains, the almost sheer yellow light tumbling through his eyelashes, the way he shouted louder when he realized that his voice would carry far through the clean fall air. I felt a huge loss of innocence. I touched his forehead with my hand. "One must believe in the reality of time," Simone Weil wrote in her *Notebooks.* "Otherwise one is just dreaming." Ronan lived, I believed, in a perpetual state of being in the now that people tried to achieve on expensive retreats, chanting and doing yoga and tweaking their nutritional habits. Was Ronan, in this way, more evolved? Did he embody a Tay-Sachs version of Nirvana, a kind of existential bliss, or was this an attempt to sprinkle glitter on a pile of shit or gloss over an absurdly tragic situation? Could it be both?

I thought of the sculptures and installations made by my friend Carrie, whom I met at the Fine Arts Work Center in Provincetown. Her work—sculptures made from paper, delicate drawings with a fierce message—creates that rare, raw enchanting experience that many of us render impossible because we analyze and criticize and categorize what we see and think and feel: wonder. A wall of paper bricks that look solid but shake and tremble when you walk by, as if you've unearthed a ghost or the walls are shifting before your eyes, all the certain made uncertain; sculptures that look impenetrable on the first glance but that are precisely, delicately made. One of her exhibits, "Breathe," was like stepping into the experience of an epiphany—a roomful of light. Each piece of paper cut by hand, the whole room fragile and fierce and paper-thin and a particular shade of yellow that, like the Sangre de Cristo aspens near Santa Fe, when gathered en masse creates an overwhelming, effervescent glow. Power and fragility combined; the color of both vulnerability and strength.

I allowed myself to imagine Ronan in a landscape of light and continuous revelation, his life lived as a series of singular moments. I wondered if in some ways, the greater loss here (or at least the most stupefying one) was mine, not Ronan's. Yes, Tay-Sachs disease would take his life; the number of his days was determined long before he could make a decision to transform the life he'd been given in one direction or another. He was denied that, but I couldn't imagine that his world was so remote, so unknowable. In this short story of his life I could not believe that he had been denied wonder. What if every moment of Ronan's life was, for him, like stepping free into a space, into a "first," into a state of wonder. Wonder that exists outside—beyond—narrative, wonder that feels like entering, again and again, for the very first time, a shining room. Dazzling but somehow expected, like the light given off by row after row of luminous trees—a blaze of impossible color. Pure experience without editorializing by the intellect. Moments that aren't folded into story but instead give off their own light. That must be the world of Ronan—his body, his mind, his heart. These thoughts comforted me.

That March, Ronan's birth month, the month that is both the start of spring and the end of winter, Rick and I met again, for the last time, with Ronan's geneticist. He never said the words "luck" or "fluke" to describe our situation. If he had, I would have left the room or possibly committed a violent crime. The doctor went on to explain that because Rick and I were both carriers of the Tay-Sachs gene (both parents must be carriers for a child to be affected), we had a one-in-four chance of having a baby *with* the disease. He asked Rick and me to lift our hands, palms facing him. "You've got two sets of genes here," he explained, "and there are four possible combinations." He closed Rick's right hand into a fist and brought it to my open-palmed right hand, and then did this several times in various combinations of palms and fists. *This* or *this* or *this* or *this*. It's as random as a doctor moving your hands around, like a genetics shell game but with unwelcome prizes waiting in your body and your blood that contain unfathomable odds.

That night I wept into the phone with a friend, asking her to do a Tarot reading or a psychic reading or *something anything something* to stop the world from spinning, to give me hope. I wailed about being unlucky and that I'd had *all* the tests and how could I possibly have this in addition to everything else and this was my worst nightmare come to life and hadn't I had enough shit to deal with and what are the odds and how would I ever trust anything again and *why why why*. She gently reminded me that I'd had a lot of good luck as well. She was right.

After I was mugged one summer in New York City, just a run-of-the-mill bag snatch (although of course it had to be my only designer bag), the cop who was driving me back to my apartment got a call on his radio. "Someone just got stabbed a few blocks from where you were," he said. "And she's dead. You're lucky, sister." When I decided to hitchhike in order to save money while traveling in Ireland, I climbed into two different cars with two different and very obviously drunk drivers; I traveled in the back of a van driven by an older man who was high and wondered if I wanted to elope in Scotland (I did not); and my final lift was with a shady twentysomething Australian who asked me, when it was just the two of us in the car on a dark road in the west of Ireland and I was now, finally, stupidly, a bit scared: "Are you a gypsy wanderer from the land of Nar?" "Of course," I stuttered, thinking Nar sounded badass, and that maybe he'd be afraid of me. "That's so fucking brilliant," he drawled, and left me off in Galway, untouched. I could go on. Would I have been unlucky had I been raped or murdered or harmed in any of these situations? And would it have been my fault? Is bad luck like a mist that falls on you or a blizzard you stumble into when the sky is otherwise clear?

The geneticist told us that if we all had our DNA analyzed, we'd freak out. We'd be horrified by the many possibilities that may await us next year, in a decade, tomorrow, next week, a moment from now.

"So it's about luck," I said.

"No," he said. "It's about life. Any of us, at any moment, could manifest something we don't expect."

I misunderstood the concept of luck by believing it existed. I didn't need to feel cursed because Ronan had a terminal illness; I was long past caring what people thought about my own disability and what may have caused it or why. We talk about luck, I think, because it makes us feel blessed (another troublesome, annoyingly "folksy" word that is spoken by a character, at some point, in every episode of Little House on the Prairie). Saying "I'm so lucky" might feel to some like a priestly incantation, the casting of a protective spell that makes people believe that they're standing on solid ground, far from catastrophe, while the unlucky folks within shouting distance squirm around in the quicksand with their cancer and diseases and dying babies; but life—not luck—will find you eventually. To say "I'm lucky" feels almost mean-spirited. It is mistaken for thankfulness, but it's not; it's smug and congratulatory, as if bad luck were a mischievous old gossipy lady with bad breath and kleptomania whom *you*, super smarty-pants you, were wise enough to kick out of your house before she slipped the family jewels into her big ugly purse while everyone else was stupid enough to let her in and serve her expensive chocolates and cups of champagne.

The snow stopped and spring flirted with Santa Fe again. I took Ronan for a walk along the arroyo path, his path, where the snow-touched mountains were visible in the near distance, flanked by the purpling hills. Some new leaves trembled on the trees. The sun was strong but not warm. Ronan quickly fell asleep, as he did in his first three months of life, when he would *only* sleep when I walked with him, and walk I did, for nearly four hours a day or more, up and down the streets of Brentwood, California, dripping with sweat while he snoozed in the front pack. He was smaller then, and when I saw my walking shadow I looked pregnant again, as if I'd swallowed a basketball. The legs and feet of a bigger Ronan cast shadows on the ground.

I stopped for a moment and gently removed his hood. I let the wind ruffle his red-blond hair and I looked at his sleeping face and I rocked him for a bit in the sun. We kept walking into a tunnel strewn with dry leaves where both our shadows disappeared and we were alone. I stood still and listened to his breath and mine. I felt a momentary flash of peace, a great still pause. T. S. Eliot's "still point of the turning world," and of course this terribly tender love, and I thought, *This is all I have to give*, and I tried with all of my strength to pass that feeling into Ronan, and then I thought, *Remember this.*

There's a scene from the film *The Curious Case of Benjamin Button* that haunts me. Unlike Kushner's child, Button was born an old man, but he, too, is aging back to death. That's some pretty crappy luck, if you're going to understand it that way, and his lover, too, was jilted out of a lifetime with him. As she, the luminous Cate Blanchett, grew old and gray and tired, he grew young and strong and super hot, that is, he turned into Brad Pitt. The accidental circumstances of his birth—his genetics—make it impossible for them to live out the dream of love: having a family and growing old together; in short, sharing the same life timeline. I was unable to forget the scene when she is rocking her former lover, now a baby, to sleep. She'll rock him until he fades completely, until he's gone. The light is soft and natural, and she rocks and rocks and rocks. She has nowhere to go, and she wouldn't dare escape that moment or the next one, or the final one; she can only rock and wait and be. She's not angry, like Frankie in *A Member of the Wedding*. No. She's gone beyond that, and her face is calm but anguished. It's not easy for her to sit there. In fact, it's the hardest thing she'll ever do, rocking through these moments. Her beloved is no longer hers, and she is no longer his. They are slipping apart. The world is loose and turning and jagged and awful and she can feel it, it won't stop, nobody can stop it and it's happening so quickly and her touch is gentle, yes, and her words are soft, of course, and she looks broken and she is, her heart is beating fire, but she still smiles at the baby as she rocks him. She comforts him, fakes calmness and serenity for his sake. In this smallest of moments she is beyond luck, beyond its frivolities and its lies. She sings, and her voice doesn't break. Because this is not the time to be fragile. This is the time to be *fierce*.

9

This is how it is with the anxious.

What will not happen is happening
all of the time.

—*Katie Ford*, "Do You Look Out the Window
Because You Feel Watched?"

Throughout the month of March I was still waking up almost every morning before the sun rose and creeping into the nursery to watch Ronan sleeping in the dark. Listening. The detached longing, an already-missing-you ache was becoming a familiar feeling. (*He woke in the dark of the woods in the leaves shivering violently. He sat up and felt about for the boy. He held his hand to his thin ribs. Warmth and movement. Heartbeat.* Cormac McCarthy, *The Road.*) As each moment with Ronan passed, I felt as if I were already redefining it, already dropping (behind? ahead?) into a state of retrospection. I worried that memory wouldn't do me any favors; that it would only make things worse. And yet we took countless pictures of Ronan, already noticing that his eyes were brighter in photos from several months before. A constant tug of war: wanting to remember, wanting to forget; wanting this to be over, and of course never wanting Ronan's life to end. How was this movement, this journey, to be mapped?

I watched Ronan's fingers twitch, listened to his heavy dinosaurish breath, admired his soft wet open mouth and his little butt shoved up in the air, and then, finally, sleepy again myself, and sad, I stretched out on the floor next to his crib and fell back to sleep. I woke to his grumbling and fussing, scratching his sheet with his little fingers no bigger than the smallest worms. Rubbing his snail ears slowly back and forth across the flannel, shaking loose whorls of sticky earwax that I lifted away from the edge of his ear with my pinky finger.

I plucked him from his crib and said, "Hello, Zoat!" He gurgled and said, "Gee." "Well, gee back at you," I said, and sat him up. I always tried to mirror his different gees, since it's the only word he said, the only spoken language we shared. I had to lay him gently on the changing table, slowly, slowly, so that his eyes wouldn't roll back into his head quite as much; it took very little to upset his balance and cause his hands to tremble and shake.

Ronan at one year was the same baby we knew at six months, only less mobile and verbal. Less bright-eyed. Having no expectations for his development was both oddly liberating and horrific. Watching for decline instead of progress. Always, always,

I was taking a backward look, which will be part of grief management until the day I die: breathing it, feeling it, eating it, knowing it, explaining it. Looking back and remembering what it was like, what it felt like, what it still felt like. Sometimes while in the shower or brushing my hair or locking my office door at school or about to take a bite of cereal or putting on my underwear I would think *I may not be a mother next year.*

This frequent, sinking feeling meant I had nothing to say to mothers with babies Ronan's age: I didn't want their pity (my well-developed radar detected that from miles away); I also didn't want to hear about what their kids were doing. But in March, Ronan was still giggling wildly enough to give himself the hiccups. Who cares if it was the painless giggle-seizures we'd been warned about? It certainly looked as if he were having fun.

Forever six months. At the end of December 2009, when I was six months pregnant and sitting with my mom in the Amtrak waiting area at Penn Station in New York, preparing to take a train to Philadelphia for a series of job interviews, we met a nine-month-old baby who was on his way to Boston with his grandmother. The baby looked enormous to me; I could not believe I would someday (*soon,* I reminded myself, *soon,* as I also felt enormous), have a person that big to prop on my hip and cart around like a living, squirming handbag wearing a diaper. I felt a cold panic spread over my body. My mom cooed at him and played peek-a-boo and made him giggle. *Well, of course,* I thought, *she knows what she's doing. She's a mom.* I was uncomfortably warm in a way-too-tight suit with the pants safety-pinned below my belly and a wool jacket with permanent underarm odor. Being pregnant was all about heat and odors, but I was too tired to do anything about it, and I knew that nobody was going to give me a job while I was pregnant, but I was going to take a train to the interview anyway. My mom flirted with the dark-haired baby for a little while longer until he grew tired of her and his grandmother waltzed him away to greet other admirers in the waiting area. Everybody loves a baby. "I love that age," my mom said, sighing. "They're just starting to talk and interact; they really become little people at nine months." I remembered this during the days after Ronan's diagnosis, when the doctors told us that all development essentially stalled out at six months before it began to unravel. Did that mean he would never even get a shot at being a little person? The thought made me want to hit my head against the wall, and sometimes I did just that.

Where would Ronan go? Certitudes had vanished. Nothing was solid. There was only my imagination, which was robust and strong and made to go the distance, to build and rebuild those "horizons of meaning" that the philosopher Hans-Georg Gadamer developed in the nineteenth century. But was it enough? I imagined Ronan treading water that shifted from dark blue to New Mexico–sky impossible. There's no color like that in the crayon box: blue to ink black to the wildly contented blue of the sea one summer along the west coast of Ireland, when I felt as if I were vacationing in the Bahamas—warm breezes, sweet sun-drenched grass, fat bees drunk with summer tumbling past our picnic blanket. The idea of staying in one place, of getting stuck, made me sad, but why? *Don't get stuck!* we tell one another. *Erase those old tapes about who you are and move on!* But to where? And to what? And why?

Why was I constantly unpacking the nature of happiness and the possibilities of Ronan's knowledge whenever I was with him? Was it his outsider existence that gave rise to these circular thoughts? *The Magic Mountain,* a thick, terrific book full of circular thoughts, seemed like a place to start searching for some answers.

A character in Thomas Mann's epic novel observes that, "Ah yes, life *is* dying—there's no sense in trying to sugarcoat it." Whenever I sent an e-mail or a text or made a phone call to one of the dragon moms they were able to sketch the quick progress of their child's life and death in a neat paragraph, a quick history, a summing up of care choices, medications, life spans. But the cracks in these stories were easy to find; apply enough pressure and the narrative fell apart—I'd yet to meet or speak with the parent of a dead child who, even decades later, didn't cry when talking about his or her son or daughter. No wrenching sobs, just quiet, necessary tears that fell while the voice stayed steady and the narrative continued. One can recite the testimonial of a war experience in a calm voice, perhaps, but nobody can control what the body knows, what it needs to release. Grief, I realized, is watery and trembling and always exists beneath the surface of real life; just a gentle touch and it's spilling everywhere. The seams are easy, too easy, to split. And that's when the real stories come out; the memories about "gee," or a certain pair of pajamas or a favorite food or toy. These babies lived lives that could not be easily recalled, but what did that mean, to quantify or render a life?

What was life? No one knew. It was aware of itself the moment it became life, that much was certain—and yet did not know what it was. Consciousness, as sensitivity to stimuli, was undoubtedly aroused to some extent at even the lowest, most undeveloped stages of its occurrence; it was impossible to tie the emergence of consciousness to any particular point in life's general or individual history—to link it, for instance, to the presence of a nervous system. The lowest animals had no nervous systems, let alone a cerebral cortex, and yet no one dared deny that they were capable of responding to stimuli. And you could anesthetize life, life itself, not just the special organs capable of the response that informs life, not just the nerves. You could temporarily suspend the responses of every speck of living matter, in both the plant and animal kingdoms, narcotize eggs and sperms with chloroform, chloral hydrate, or morphine. Consciousness of self was an inherent function of matter once it was organized as life, and if that function was enhanced it turned against the organism that bore it, strove to fathom and explain the very phenomenon that produced it, a hope-filled and hopeless striving of life to comprehend itself, as if nature were rummaging to find itself in itself—ultimately to no avail, since nature cannot be reduced to comprehension, nor in the end can life listen to itself. (From *The Magic Mountain*)

Mann, of course, in this very serious-sounding, vaguely scientific passage, was influenced by Hegel's phenomenological theories: things become what they are during the process of becoming what they are; in other words, all life forms are forged in the fire of a never-ending, tumbling-forward-and-behind-and-sideways process. They don't just land at an end point, whole and complete, and they never stop changing. They never *arrive*. More than a decade ago I sat in a sun-filled classroom at Harvard and wrangled grumpily with Hegel and what his elaborate system of thinking, which required whole pages of charts and graphs to sort out, had to do with theology, life, or really anything at all. *Didn't this dude have anything else to do with his time?* I wondered, and waited impatiently for us to get to Nietzsche in the course schedule, the guy who'd famously announced that God was dead, the cool-grunge hipster philosopher of the nineteenth century who wrote in an exuberant, fascinating prose style. Anyone who has ever trudged through one of Hegel's muddy, dense passages of prose may understand this frustration.

And yet Mann and Hegel were onto something. What the hell is life? (*That, finally, is all it means to be alive: to be able to die.—*

J. M. Coetzee.) How do we recognize it, protect it and, finally, as we are all asked (that is, forced to do), let it go? Can it just be life without knowledge of its lifeness? And, in our case, mine and Rick's, how would we let life go for someone else, for our favorite person, for our child, for our *baby*?

Rick and I had this ridiculous conversation on a regular basis:

"He's the best little boy, the sweetest little dude. He's a baby!"

"He's the best baby in the world, the best and sweetest boy."

"Best baby."

"Our baby, the only baby."

"We love our little guy, the little baby."

On and on it went like this, back and forth between the two of us, day after day, and when we were not actually having this conversation with each other, we were having it with ourselves. And the thing is, it was absolutely true. He was ours; he was the best. It was also about all we could say, because he would always be a baby, but would he ever really get to *live*?

What can be learned from a dying baby?

In the spring of 2011, not long after Ronan's first birthday, a news story made headlines around the world—a story that forced me to examine these quality-of-life questions more deliberately and deeply. Father Pavone was a priest who helped facilitate the transfer of Baby Joseph, a terminally ill baby, from a Canadian hospital to a medical center in St. Louis so that Joseph could receive additional treatment to prolong his life. Joseph's Canadian doctors had refused to treat him because he was in a vegetative state. Father Pavone stated that the child, the baby, provided a "teaching moment for our whole culture" about the value of life. I couldn't agree more, although I believe the issue may be less about *value* than it is about *quality*.

This was not just semantics. The quick degeneration of Ronan's brain tissue due to the lack of hex-A, a crucial enzyme, meant that all his bodily systems would be irrevocably compromised by the age of two, resulting in a gradual disconnect from the faculties that make life livable: movement, vision, taste, touch, sound. Although Baby Joseph's illness (and he is always a Baby, not just a Joseph) was never specifically named, it didn't sound dissimilar to Tay-Sachs in terms of severity and resistance to known treatments. If only Ronan's body was devastated but his brain was intact, if he had the smallest foothold in any mental process or physical experience, would Rick and I do everything possible to keep him alive? Absolutely. Even now we could make choices, as Joseph's parents and their posse of priests did, to keep his heart beating, but our son—as we know him, as a person—would be gone. After exhaustive, wrenching conversations Rick and I decided to believe (and belief is always a decision; Father Pavone got that part right) that using extraordinary measures to maintain Ronan's future life in a vegetative state with no possibility of recovery would constitute cruelty. As Ronan's parents, we understood that our obligations to him were to maintain his quality of life, and to help him die with dignity, without pain, and in our home. *Life is about living,* we said, playing with Baby Ronan, our baby, the little baby, our little dude. *Yes, yes. We're making the right choice.* But what did that mean, *life is about living*? What did it mean *really*? Was I saying that when my child could no longer *think,* that he was no longer a person? That, too, was a complicated question.

There were many levels to Baby Joseph's case, and that the courts should not be able to decide the fate of any child with parents to speak for him or her seems obvious. I empathized with Baby Joseph's parents in a raw and gut-wrenching way. Losing a child (or, in our case, preparing for that loss over the course of several years) is sheer hell; I disagreed with Joseph's parents—without judging them—while simultaneously indict-ing a culture determined to deny death to the point of grasping at any methods that might prolong "life" without an in-depth exploration as to what it is we're talking about.

Our family faced gruesome choices: how would we know when Ronan's quality of life had diminished to the point where letting him go was the more humane option? Was it when he stopped swallowing and vocalizing, when he could no longer see us or experience our loving touch? Any of these eventuali-ties might coincide with the option for a feeding tube (the most likely first intervention) or they might not. These decisions are made more emotionally complicated by the fact that the medi-cal community in this country has become expert at prolong-ing life to the point of being unwilling or unable to engage in any nuanced discussion about what it is they're saving. With the exception of hospice, doctors offer little help to parents who are navigating this bleak terrain.

Case study: The neurologist/pediatrician/geneticist felt that the choice *not* to insert a feeding tube for a child with a "terminal illness" was "ridiculous." Some other (in all fairness, solicited) advice: "I wouldn't want to starve to death." "We don't let babies starve to death in this country." "Feeding tubes are easy." So the decision to reject a feeding tube was tantamount to . . . murder?

"But," I countered, "we're not talking about a starving child living in some country where food is not available and that's why they're starving, are we?"

A brief pause. This doctor knew where I was going. I didn't like being called a murderess. "No," he said finally.

When I worked for a world relief organization in Geneva, I met women whose children had died from malnutrition, diarrhea, typhoid, war-related violence, meningitis, malaria, botched abortions, fevers and the flu. In Ronan's case it wasn't an issue of a growling stomach, a bloated belly. He had not contracted a disease that was a direct result of living in conditions of squalor and forced poverty.

A nurse put Ronan's index finger in a tiny machine to take his pulse. He found this amusing and squealed at her.

"So, if the body is no longer able to eat, it's kind of like an animal who stops eating and then goes out under a tree and dies," I said. "It's a sign. It's nature stepping in to take over."

"All good," the nurse said, and let Ronan's finger slip free. He looked up at her and smiled as if he wanted her to do it again.

"But we're not talking about dogs, we're talking about people, and a feeding tube is easy," the doctor continued. The reference to dogs upset and alarmed me. I felt my face getting hot; I was ready to go to war (with him, with anyone). But he was also making his point.

A feeding tube was "easy." It may extend life by six months or longer, but this paved the way to other, more serious interventions that Rick and I would not consider, because all the while the brain was fading, fading, fading, and then it was gone. No, it wasn't just an ability to think that made life, it was eating, breathing, moving, hearing, seeing. That might coincide with the option for a feeding tube or it might not. No crystal balls, sadly. When he couldn't interact or hear or feel or see us, was it just a beating heart we were saving, and why?

When my memoir about growing up with a disability was published in 2007, I was asked to comment on the situation with Terri Schiavo, who was on life support at the time and whose condition galvanized a national debate about quality-of-life issues the way Baby Joseph's did, however briefly. I got huffy and offended, because how dare they ask a disabled woman, just because she's disabled, about a woman who is in a vegetative state, as if these two situations are equivalent? After Ronan's diagnosis and all of this torturous thinking, I had plenty to say. It's an issue of whether or not a person—Baby Ronan or Baby

Joseph or any person—will be alive in the world—reacting to it, aware of it, *in* it in any significant way at all.

Three hours later, after this initial encounter with doctors, we were handed this competing worldview from the hospice doctor: "When the body can no longer feed itself, sometimes it is uncomfortable to provide nourishment. It's the body's way of shutting down."

"So it's not cruel, right?" I asked. The room was well lit but not with fluorescent lights; it was borderline cheery and homey. We sat around a mission-style wooden table. It felt as if we were all sitting down together, not so much to discuss a disease but to discuss our baby, this person Rick and I loved more than any other person in the world, including each other. I half expected a mariachi band to start playing or someone to bustle over and ask if we'd like to order a margarita.

"It is not," he said, and then, looking right at me, as if he knew I needed to hear it, he repeated, "It is absolutely not cruel. It's what the body does; it knows what to do. And so do we. We know how to help people die." I handed Ronan to Rick and put my head in my hands and sobbed.

Hospice care refers to terminal illnesses as "life-limiting" diseases. The head nurse wore a floor-length velvet skirt and blond bangs. Another gave Ronan a blinking light that we quickly named his Ronan-Wan-Kenobi life saber. In this room in the hospital's pediatric wing, the sun lined the nurses' faces; they wore IDs on lanyards that made me think of my years as a camp counselor and the way I once sternly instructed the kids in my charge: "Don't. Swing. Your. Lanyards!"—and I had a sharp pang in my gut, wishing Ronan would grow up to be one of those slouchy, grumpy kids on the cusp of adolescence, a kid with acne and attitude and a budding libido that excited and confused him. Liberated from the sharp angles and cold tile floors of the Mind Center, the energy here was muted, respectful and solemn, but also wildly celebratory in a way that was almost euphoric. There were circus posters on the walls and padded chairs to sit on. The physical therapist gave us a blanket made by some Lutheran women in Albuquerque. I could easily picture them sitting around a long table in a spic-and-span church basement that smelled of bleach and sugar, eating *krumkaka* and sipping weak percolated black coffee, chattering away. Nobody said, "I'm sorry." What they did say: "This is a journey, and we are proud to be on it with you." I believed them. It was almost as if we had all gotten together and said, "Well, we're all going to die. Isn't it a relief?" *One usually begins to pose the question of the meaning of life and reflect on it in a fundamental way when one is suddenly ambushed and overpowered by a painful question: "And what next?" A question essentially the same as the question "So what?"* Václav Havel writing from prison, August 15, 1981. So now what?

That afternoon we learned that kids are dying all over the state as they are all over the world, every moment, all the time. Kids dying from leukemia, from other metabolic disorders that are similar to Tay-Sachs and have the same end result, from bone marrow cancer and liver and kidney disease, from neglect and abuse and violence and the effects of wrenching poverty. Kids and babies die, but in our world of the "miracles" of modern medicine we don't expect it, we say it's "wrong," we kick and rail against it. We say "tragic." We ask, *How can this be happening?*

So were the Canadian doctors who refused to perform a procedure that had no possibility of leading to Baby Joseph's recovery passing judgment on the *value* of his brief life as the Priests for Life insisted? No, they were passing judgment on the *quality* of his life. Nobody was debating whether or not Baby Joseph's life was valuable—to his parents and to the world. But the controversy surrounding this single baby gave rise to difficult questions that all of us, parents or otherwise, work hard to avoid considering: What standards are we willing to use in order to judge the quality of any particular life? What kind of life am I willing to subject my baby to?

As a mother I was charged with making impossible decisions about my child's right to life, and I argue that it was Ronan's right to live as fully as possible, in the world, with at least some of his faculties intact, and that it was my burden and my right to determine when his quality of life had become irretrievably compromised. When my son's brain was devastated and his body destroyed by this disease, to refuse to prolong his life through medical intervention would say nothing about how valuable he was to me, or how impossible it would be to quantify his loss.

The first time Rick and I met with Ronan's care team at the Children's Hospital—an arduous day of one pediatrician, one neurologist, three hospice nurses, one hospice doctor and one physical therapist—Rick was nervous and talked a lot; I was thirsty and starving but almost gagged when I tried to drink the lemonade that seconds before I'd been desperate to guzzle. Between meetings with the members of our mighty crew we fed Ronan in the hospital cafeteria and picked at a few stale bagels. "How can you eat?" I asked Rick. I felt like punching him, punching someone.

He gave me a sad, bewildered look, a slight smile, and said, "I'm like a dog. I'll eat through anything." He took three bites, one after the other.

"You eat like a prisoner," I said unkindly. "This isn't a fucking prison," I said, but as soon as I said this, I realized that it felt like one. He ignored me. I offered an insincere apology and stared out the windows at people in the courtyard: nurses eating salads and pointing plastic forks at one another to make a point; a drug company representative (his briefcase was an advertisement) talking to a beleaguered-looking doctor; another seemingly depressed family with a six-year-old who didn't look sick, but then who knew?

After an entire day spent discussing Ronan's end-of-life options, I talked for the next few days, for hours and hours, with three different mothers who did not use feeding tubes and whose children died before age three. I kept saying, *Yes, that's how we feel. Exactly, exactly! What are we prolonging? I know, I know.* I wanted someone to tell me that we were making the right choice. I finally turned off my phone minutes before another scheduled phone chat with a mom. I wanted to take a nap, eat one of Rick's gourmet dinners, go to my friend Nouf's birthday party and drink too much sparkling wine. All of which I did.

We could only do for Ronan what we would do for ourselves: Rick and I didn't want tubes even waved around in our vicinity; we were not, as the saying goes, "bitter enders." With that in mind, we tried to make these absurd decisions for our son. The stakes couldn't have been any higher, and I felt totally unprepared for the reality of his death, even as I often longed for it, if only to release him from suffering.

Is it Christianity that makes this discussion about death such a chore? Traditional imagery envisions life versus death as a confrontation of warring factions, a battlefield struggle. In *Life After Death*, the theologian T. A. Kantonen writes, "Christian faith not only affirms fully the reality of death but also looks upon death as an enemy to be overcome. Then it goes on to affirm that in the conflict between life and death the decisive battle has already been fought and won." A militaristic myth of salvation, then, with Christ as the quartermaster, the celebrated general with his saints marching on for triumph and plunder. Yet another overcomer narrative. Great.

For many people the concept of heaven is a massive comfort. This didn't work for me: I couldn't picture Ronan floating, cherubic, into the arms of the grandmother and grandfather I'd never met, or hugging and kissing all the people I'd loved who had died, as if I could determine a roomful of my loved ones and magically place him there in the middle of a celestial family reunion of Rapps and Gormans and Slagells and Dohertys and Kakaras: Ronan ex machina. Would these people even enjoy being in proximity to one another in heaven or anywhere else? How would they recognize one another and what age would they be? Does heaven have rooms or puffy cloud condos and stringy cloud strip malls or what?

Buddhist theories discuss death as the final gateway of life, a threshold. I liked this idea, as well as the image of a doorway; it helped me imagine accompanying Ronan right up to that line, that threshold, even if we could not cross over it with him. In this country, in this culture, we have become exceptionally good at "saving" lives, but we are "rubbish," as my friend Emily would say, in terms of understanding what the hell that means. What are we saving and why? Who gets to make the choice? How do you respond ethically when you are asked to make the choice for someone else, for your child, for your baby whose life is, literally, in your hands?

At the hospital, as we were wrapping up our discussion about Ronan's end-of-life care, the head hospice doctor, who wasn't harried like most doctors—in fact he seemed to have all the time in the world—said, "We know how to help babies with life-limiting diseases." Is "life-limiting" just a silly, euphemistic way of saying "terminal/about to die/totally doomed"? Are these tweaks in language similar to the discussion of "differently abled" *and* "handicapable" versus "handicapped," "crippled" and "disabled"? Is it just semantics? Maybe, but I liked the idea that "life" was at least acknowledged in the hospice

version of Ronan's condition, even though these folks are the
ones who will be helping us prepare for his death. Life and
death together. The ultimate pairing. Truly the only one that
matters.

"We have to ask, at every stage and with every possible intervention," the doctor went on, "what is this for? What does it
lead to? What kind of a life is he living?" In other words, if the
life is truly limited, when there is no cure, then what are we
prolonging? He was wearing a blue shirt. His hands were square
and strong, builder's hands; he had a fireman's muscled arms.
A doctor—a man—who helps people die. *How does he feel in
this body right now?* His job was to help us answer these questions
about Ronan and make decisions about next steps. We shook
his hand and he left the room. I thought, *The next time I see that
doctor Ronan will be dying, and not just in the abstract but for real.*

The meaning of Ronan's life was not to teach me; we often
say this about people who defy our notions of normal and I
find it pathetic, patronizing, and a way of distancing ourselves
from our own fragile bodies and tenuous lives. I don't believe
that disabled people exist to teach people life stories—that is
not their purpose; it isn't anyone's purpose. We are not "the
disabled," some shapeless, teeming mass of nonnormative bodies designed for teaching purposes, like some kind of specially
designed pedagogical barbarian horde.

So Ronan would have his own path that had nothing to do
with me, and I would try to understand it in my limited way.
We are creatures, all of us, growing, shifting, moving, but never

really arriving. I was thankful to Hegel for making his nerdy, complicated graphs and diagrams about Spirit. Thinking about that—and not a Disneyfied version of the shoebox heaven, with a cutout Jesus glued to a Popsicle stick and flanked by white construction-paper angels sprinkled with glitter, the one many of us were encouraged to imagine in Sunday school—was helping me.

And Ronan was making me think, yes, and he was making me think about thinking (Hegel would be pleased), but my task as his myth writer was still to understand my son as a person and a being who was independent of me and yet dependent on my actions, my attention, my love. I would not and will never do him the disservice of regarding him as an angel or telling myself that God had "other" plans for him, and for me. My plan was simple and yet impossible: to go with him as far as I could along this journey that we call life, to be with him as deeply as I could from moment to moment, and then to let him go.

10

Grief is:

    An empty pillow book

    Waiting for someone to change the subject

    Ink spilled on white pants or a white sheet: ink from a
        pen, ink from a squid, blue-black and slimy

    Sighing a lot

    Feeling naked in private and feeling private in public

    Running amok

    Bulimic, anorexic, gluttonous, abstemious and
        possessed of other varying appetites

    Flammable

    Responding to a simple question with a trilogy,
        already a bestseller in online preorders

    The sea, wherever it is found

A blister slowly shaping itself to the bottom of a foot

Turbulence in an airplane as soon as you are handed a
cup of hot coffee or tomato juice or, if flying
internationally in coach/tourist class, a plastic cup
full of red wine

A hand on an ass when it is not welcome

Long nails in need of clipping

Airport food

A sudden nosebleed

Slutty

Faithful to the last

History misspelled by an accidental keystroke:
"shitory"

An eight-hour time change every five minutes

Standing on a table while people discuss your faults,
a few strengths

Impulsive and cantankerous: a terrible travel
companion

Time. All clocks. Every watch, even Swiss made

A stuffed panda with a single ear, forgotten on a bus,
slumped over like a sleeping passenger

A stereotypical image of a dictator: broad shoulders
tapering to a narrow waist, a jagged ponytail with
furiously splitting ends, busy eyes, bushy eyebrows

A dog that barks all night until it is kicked

Green and slippery, like the truth, like a lie

A bird halfway between the lowly pigeon and the self-
    righteous hawk, circling

A story by Kafka

Endlessly resourceful

A half-read book

Worrying about a beloved friend staying in Paris in a
    rented flat. Is the roof secure? Is there rain in the
    forecast? Did she find milk at the store? What is she
    eating?

An endless conversation with past and future selves in
    shouts and whispers

An unwashed nightgown on a dirty hook

Sudden chatter of sunlight, everywhere

A skinny rat swimming past a subway car during a
    rainstorm, car stalled out and bobbing

Trash from the upstairs neighbors flying past your
    window

Not telling you anything

Chasing a coin across the floor before it drops out of
    reach

Amateur at everything

An unfinished letter

Stinky air fresheners with names like "Summer
    Daffodil" and "Sporty Grape"

A vacation in the middle of the ocean, crappy raft
    optional

The phrases "getting accustomed" and "being brave"
    and "you're my hero"
A shoddy translation
A stack of postcards from places you've never been
    bound with a rubber band, discovered in the
    bedside drawer of your favorite friend

11

The moment
before joy is horizonless. What falls
falls surrounded by what's falling.

—Philip Pardi, "Sonata"

In those winter and early spring months of 2011, I was writing about Ronan and he was still alive. As a teacher of writing, I had in the past yammered on at length about the importance of gaining objectivity about a situation drawn from real life—especially a deeply personal or emotionally difficult one—in order to render it effectively without sentimentality or nostalgia. I chucked that piece of advice, because after Ronan's diagnosis I found the opposite to be true. I wrote with my son in my lap or within arm's reach. I wrote while looking right at him, in the middle of feeding him, talking to him, wiping his mouth, ruffling the fuzzy hair on the back of his head. I wrote in a rage, in tears, through laughter, exhaustion and bizarre moments of euphoria. For many years I had a quote, given to me by a writing professor in graduate school, pinned above my desk: *Write with blood.* I thought it sounded serious and writerly. After I started writing Ronan's story, I finally understood what it meant and took it down. The advice was too resonant, too true, and I didn't need it anymore.

Many writers have written beautifully about grief while in the raw early stages of it (Joyce Carol Oates, Megan O'Rourke, Robin Romm and many others); grief, this extreme experience, forces a writer to draw on her deepest resources, and such a dive demands so much work that what comes up must be heaved onto the page almost immediately; otherwise it might eat the thinker alive, drown them. (*It steadies me to tell these things.* From "Settings," by Seamus Heaney.) Or at least that's how I felt. You can eat fire for only so long, and then you've got to spit it out in another form or risk the burn.

But as I pulled book after book from my bookshelves, look-ing for how various writers told their grief stories, I'd read a few pages and throw them on the floor. My skin prickled with mean-spirited annoyance and then I felt myself getting *angry.* I was vibrating with rage. Many of the books were about dead spouses, dying parents, dying dogs. *My loss is different,* I thought. *My loss is worse,* I thought. I felt sick to my stomach, sat down on the floor, put my head in my hands and thought, *Wait . . .*

My initial reaction to these books, knee-jerk and overly emotional, automatically assumed the existence of a ladder of loss and a method for placing a person's sadness on a particular rung. So . . . what, on the lower rung the loss of a pet fish? On the upper rung the loss of a parent, a spouse or a child? *Yes*, you might say, *just like that*. Okay, but what if the fish belonged to a five-year-old, and it was his first experience with death and you were charged with explaining what had happened and what it meant while Goldy bobbed in the water of his bowl cum grave? What if the parent or spouse or baby was suffering for years or months or even for just one minute, then what? Bumped down a few rungs on the ladder? This idea that there existed a hierarchy, a "my grief is more grievous than yours" method of ranking, with those at the top having a more gut-wrenching, authentically earth-shaking experience while those on the lower rungs were—what? Just super, super sad?—was obviously ludicrous, and I was reluctantly forced to admit my shortsighted and simplistic response.

Loss, like any profound human experience, is not quantifiable—if there did exist a competition for grief, who would want to win it? This is precisely why grief, like love and any other foundational, deceptively simple human emotion or state of being, is the terrain of artists. And it is a writer's even more specific job to give voice to loss in whatever ways she can, to give shape to this unspeakable, impermeable reality beneath all other realities. Elizabeth Bishop's famous poem "One Loss" speaks precisely to this fact. There are not a handful of losses to master, but one; not a tangled batch of emotions to understand, just the one: grief.

When I emerged from those first thunderous days after

Ronan's diagnosis, I began to write because it felt like the only thing I was able to do. I could not have been more surprised, and I was actually embarrassed. I wanted to *write*? Really? Losing my child, an experience already against the expected natural order of things, would be my first experience of a loss of this magnitude (but there again—what do I mean by that? That pesky ranking system), and I had expectations about what a "grieving person" does, says, feels, how they act, what they *do*. Wasn't I supposed to run barefoot through the streets in my nightdress and shriek and howl and pull my hair out? I did a version of this, only indoors. But one can maintain that for only so long. Eventually I sat up and thought, *Yes, this is apocalyptic and world ending*, but also, *leave me alone, get out of my way, I've got work to do, let me write.*

Why? I'd been disconnected from my writing life for years, and during that time I'd been preaching in writing classes about the importance of establishing objective distance from difficult life stories before trying to render them on the page. Or, and I quote myself here, "otherwise those stories can be heavy loads for the reader to lift." "Writing," I prattled on, "should not be therapeutic; it's not therapy; it's *art*." Now I had my own monstrous load to haul around, and although I still believed that it couldn't be all doomsday and sadness in the writing, even if that was how the heart felt, I found my advice, and my chirping on about "paper doll physics"—which has nothing to do with physics but everything to do with how you separate the "I" on the page from the "I" doing the writing (and yes, a physical paper doll is involved as an illustration)—naive at best, but borderline self-righteous and wholly uneducated in the vicissitudes of grief. In those first hellish weeks, I had to write; that was all there was. That was living. (My friend Lisa, also a writer and one schooled in the ways of grief, called me every day. *Write!* she urged. *Do it right now!*)

That's all very dramatic, I thought, writing with Ronan snuggled into my armpit, *but what does writing do?* It was not saving Ronan in the literal sense (if only if only if only) because nothing could, and it wouldn't save anyone else and it certainly wasn't going to save the world. What about my intentions? Was I trying to "save" Ronan, as if turning his story into a project would make the situation less "true" and therefore easier to bear? Yes and no. Writers scribbling in the midst of grief have noted the ways in which writing about the experience from the inside creates something new, namely, a safe or safe-ish place to rest. A net, a landing point, a dock from which to view the turbulent and troubled water without having to wade in it every moment of every day. In a word: relief. The act of creation forces the creator to establish a new world with new rules and structure and form, an act that is sustaining not only in an emotional and a human way *but also in an artistic way.* This last point is key; yes, these grieving writers journaled and documented their day-to-day lives, all those singular moments, but they also went back and shaped their words. They did the work of revision, they wrestled with language and form. Plunked down into a situation in which they were entirely helpless, they found something to *do*, not to distract themselves from the situation but to look it straight in the face as artists, like it or not, are required to do. Otherwise, what are we doing?

After those first few weeks of blackness and bouncing back and forth in the void, I realized that I didn't want to be coddled or protected from the wild unpredictability of my feelings. I wanted to work, laugh, write, be, *live*. People fully expected the weeping and gnashing of teeth, but they also expected the griever to get over it already. Grief makes people feel awkward, in part because we've been trained to say things like "I can't imagine" and "Somehow you'll get past it" (as in step around it as if it were sidewalk dog doo-doo? Unlikely) and "keep yourself busy," all these useless sayings that stem from the death phobia that permeates our culture. And, I would argue, because grief is so intimate and unwieldy and, like individual experiences of pain, truly unknowable, even to the person walking or stumbling through it, it can be difficult to make a connection with someone in the midst of it, even if that person is your spouse, your mother or your best friend, or even yourself.

We all avoid death—we don't want to see it, talk about it or think about it. But digging into the experience of loss is not only deeply profound but artistically, at some points, absolutely electric. People want (and sometimes encourage) the griever to numb it or erase it or at the very least ignore it, and all a writer can think to do is to pull it closer and wrap her arms around it and dig in her fingernails and *hang on*. "Don't write if you don't feel up to it," people cautioned me when I told them I had started to write about Ronan. But it didn't matter if I felt "up" to it. It was my responsibility; it was my job. It ordered chaos, focused energy, provided a way of "bearing up" that no period of restfulness could possibly accomplish. In other words, rendering loss was a way of honoring life. I brought my whole self to the page and used my whole heart to consider what I was writing. I let go of my old fears about how my work would be received, how *I* was or would be received, and just created. There was nowhere to go inside Ronan's diagnosis, but on the page my mind could move, and I was, for that brief period of time—an hour, four hours, three minutes, five seconds—free.

So you might say that I was and still am compelled to write, called to write, forced to write. Who is doing the calling?

God?

Pastors and priests and other holy folks and men and women of the cloth (I love this expression because it brings to mind loincloths, as if pastors were early hunter-gatherers, but of souls instead of big game) are "called" to their vocations. It sounds nice, but when your pastor dad is "called" to middle-of-nowhere Nebraska when you're a bratty fourteen-year-old, the romance of the idea fizzles quickly (as does the playfulness of the loincloth imagery). Saint Paul, née Saul, had a conversion experience akin to a seizure of the soul and spirit that prompted him to change his entire life and write lots and lots of letters. Martin Luther was struck by a violent lightning force of a calling that had him trembling on his fat knees on a dirt road somewhere in rural Germany, questioning all that he had previously so ardently believed in. Out of this experience he crafted Lutheranism. John Calvin believed that our vocations were preordained by God. Do lawyers have such melodramatic vocational callings? Plumbers? Maids? Editors? CEOs?

In Frances Sherwood's novel *Vindication,* about the life of pioneering feminist Mary Wollstonecraft, there's a scene in which Mary is trying to puzzle out the age-old "why bad things happen to good people" conundrum. Why do some people receive soft down pillows and chocolates and other people are left to battle a constant shit storm? For answers she turns to Mr. Price, her pastor, her mentor and, most important, the first and only gentle man she's ever known, a man who believes that women—and especially Mary—can have a life of the mind and that her wholly original ideas will teach and inspire and change people.

"Let God be the judge," Mr. Price cautioned. "Things happen for a reason."

"Bad things?"

"Sometimes. We learn from them."

Mrs. Price nodded in agreement.

"Tell me," Mary insisted, "is there a reason for a child's death? What does a dead child learn?"

Mr. Price has no pithy answer for this, and I doubt Calvin would either—his children all died in infancy. But later in Sherwood's novel, which pulls no punches and can be rough going, this portrait of the artist as a young woman makes clear that being a brilliant thinker cost the tormented, mercurial and impulsive Wollstonecraft; her inner and outer lives were constantly at odds. After a second suicide attempt, Mary awakens on the bank of the Thames, having just been rescued from the water. This event marks a kind of rebirth for her, an awakening.

"We must go on living," Mary concluded. "It is our duty."

Is it enough? "What did you do to manage it?" I asked other dragon moms, thinking about how the next few years of my life would roll out. "Make memories," they advised. For some that meant going to Disneyland or the Bahamas with their families. I understood both approaches, but they didn't resonate with me. "We sat on the couch a lot," one mom, Sharon, told me, about her time with her son Harry, who died of Tay-Sachs when he was two and a half. "That's what I remember most." That spoke to me. I spend (and have spent) a great deal of my life sitting on couches—reading, writing and talking on the phone. During my college summer vacations, when I wasn't peddling overpriced bras and matching panties at the lingerie store in the mall or selling hiking boots and waterproof watches at the sporting goods store on the other floor of the mall, I parked my book-hungry self on the blue-flowered couch in my parents' living room and got up only for meals, the mail, the Cher exercise video that I did once a day and the nightly jabberfest with my closest friends on the phone in my dad's basement office, where I installed myself on an equally comfortable yet rattier couch.

When I sat writing with Ronan on the couch, there existed inside this helpless, frantic sadness exquisite moments of pristine happiness and an almost-perfect peace. I propped him against my chest and circled my arms around him to get to the keyboard on my laptop. I stared at him and tickled him and kissed him and wished that my words, anything, could save him. But no, writing would not save Ronan. *But,* I thought, *it might save me.*

12

At the end of March I traveled to Boston to attend the National Tay-Sachs and Allied Disorders Association family conference, where I met other children like Ronan and other mothers in my situation. I stayed with friends I'd known for fifteen years. In the mornings I woke to the sound of Weber's three-year-old daughter, Violet, knocking on my door. In the afternoons I held the hands of kids with Tay-Sachs, Sandhoff, Canavan and other terminal diseases. I missed Ronan and longed to hold him. On the way to the airport after the conference ended, I told my friend Kate that it was almost impossible to imagine feeling this way forever, this ache. She put one arm around me and drove with one hand.

After a brief scare over the lack of a ticket at Logan, and a very nice woman who finally fixed the problem for exactly $967 less than she was supposed to, I was waiting at the gate when a woman began crying hysterically and screaming, saying *You can't do this to me again. You're ruining my life. Oh my God, I can't believe this.* I literally thought somebody had died. As it turned out, the woman had been told she needed to check her luggage because the overhead bins were full, but the last time she'd flown the airline had ruined her laptop. I had zero sympathy for her as she boarded the plane in a teary huff. I watched her sit down in the row in front of me, still squalling, still hysterical, and thought about offering her a Xanax or perhaps the weekend schedule for the Tay-Sachs family conference: symptom management, secretion control, choosing an end-of-life plan, memorials, support groups for grieving parents at different stages of a terminal disease.

The man sitting next to me pointed at the back of her seat and mouthed, "Freak." I nodded. The woman sitting next to her had a gentler response. She asked the woman if she was okay, handed her a tissue, and then the real story came out. For years the crying woman had been homeless, jobless, and her computer, her laptop, the one thing that had allowed her some freedom, some ability to look for jobs, had been ruined when she flew home for a family funeral with money a friend had given her as a gift. The man next to me was still chuckling, but I was not. I was no longer in the mood for his jeers or my complicity in them moments before. I thought about what people might say about Ronan at the later stages, some of the names they might call him, the way I had used the word "retarded" in the past; the way people regard difference, including mine—staring at me when I wore shorts, letting their jaws drop at public pools when I took the leg off, the great anxiety about the body during any sexual encounter. The great "reveal" of showing another person *I am not what you thought; I am this.* And I thought, *No, she's not a freak; she's someone's child, and beyond that she's a person.*

Four hours later and the air on the jetway was like heavy cake. Texas. The Dallas airport again, desperately trying to be like Heathrow: same font used for the signs, same glossy stores lining the terminals, arrows directing you to the "toilets" instead of the restrooms. Through the windows of the above-ground Skylink train whisking between terminals, the lights of the city dripped in the thick sky. I sat near the front of the train as if it were a carnival ride, and I thought about all the sick kids I'd met during the weekend in Boston, where I'd held so many tiny hands.

In Santa Fe one morning I was becoming irritated by the loud group of retirees sitting next to me at the coffee shop when one of the men stood up and said, "Okay, it's chemo day for me, so I'll see you later!" and strolled away. We know so little about people's lives, about what they go through. At least at the family conference, where we'd huddled together and tried to figure out how to manage and eventually eliminate all these terrible insane diseases, everything was out in the open— all the misery, gallows humor, joy, fear, dread. As one mother said, "People talk about living each day as if it were your last, but that's a completely exhausting way to live." This desire to pack the days full of meaning and memory was another kind of ambition: there was always something more you could say, do, become, always a reach for the "what next?" Sitting with Ronan on the couch I often thought, *How can I make this moment more precious?* and then I'd realize with a sense of panic that no additional meaning needed to be sought or found. This was all there was. *But still*, I would think, *What if I can't remember the way his hands feel, his hair. What if I forget how he smells? The sound of his laugh? The shape of his two front teeth?* Time was both too contracted and forever seeming. (From Pablo Neruda: *"I don't have enough time to celebrate your hair."*)

There are many horrible things about living with a terminally ill child, but the hardest is the way in which our parenting approach approximates an old archetypal story but without the redemptive ending: when your child is dying and there is no treatment or cure, it feels as though you are sending him or her out into the wilderness, only there is no returning from this particular exile. Nobody is passed over. Nobody is freed. The faces of those children and their parents were brave and beautiful because they were singular faces, unique. The parents knew their children's bodies and needs on every level; they learned to read the subtlest cues; they found moments, even in the later stages of the disease, when elements of the child's personality burst through.

And now I knew their stories, their desperately human stories that are the worst kind of sad, but in some moments, absolutely laugh-out-loud funny: one little girl with Tay-Sachs who, until the end of her life, always had a grumble for the most problematic family member; another little boy who used to laugh at inappropriate moments and make everyone else laugh, too, and when they hadn't expected it. What these parents did—what Rick and I did—was as sacred as it was misunderstood, and very often ignored.

There was something profound and liberating about naming the unspeakable, giving it voice, letting it live in a room, stretch its legs, burp, be obnoxious. I could sit in a support group and talk about "growing into a diagnosis" and possible approaches to pulmonary care. I could discuss studies proving that when people can no longer eat, when their bodies shut down, there occurs an incredible physical euphoria that is the opposite of pain or discomfort. And then someone would tell a joke. And then someone would tell the story about the final days with his or her child, and the importance of hospice care and night nursing. He might erupt into tears or she might speak carefully in a stoic, controlled voice. Sitting in circles, loving their kids, suctioning lungs or feeding or rocking or comforting, all of those people were children once, they were or still are somebody's child and then they were parents in a terrible situation and they were fierce. Their children had the most powerful claim on them. And all of them had a claim on me.

This is it: having a terminally ill child has, in many ways, ruined my life because Ronan will die. But talking with these parents helped me strategize about how I might survive his death; with these moms and dads I discussed practical considerations (doctors, care options, alternative treatments) as well as all the impractical considerations (how to be strong and hopeful in the face of hopelessness): the steep learning curve of all I'd need to learn. More than anything else, however, each face in that circle, infant or adult or otherwise, taught me that learning how to live with death—that final wilderness from which none of us returns—was also about learning how to *live*.

13

God resolved at the outset that He wanted
every human to participate in the afterlife.
But the plans weren't thought out to
completion, and immediately He began to
run up against some confusion about age.
How old should each person be in the
afterlife? Should this grandmother exist
here at her death, or should she be allowed
to live as a young woman, recognizable to
her first lover but not to her
granddaughter?

—David Eagleman, "Prism," in *Sum:
Tales of the Afterlives*

After I returned from the conference in Boston, I woke up
and held my son for a long, long time. I'd missed him terribly for those three days. Sitting on the couch, Ronan and

I flipped through his art cards from Dr. Janet—black-and-white sketches of a panda, a ring-tailed lemur, an anteater, a penguin—as I composed a long-overdue list of thank-you notes that needed to be written for his many birthday gifts. His spasticity had worsened, his hands springing together when he was on his back as if he were holding magnets in his palms or moving under water. When I thought about the effort it took for him to reach out and turn the pages of a soft book, I wanted to squeeze him and never let him go. But I let him grunt and reach because it was what he wanted to do. Even a dying baby can have ambitions of a kind, and I allowed him his.

Sometimes it felt possible to exist in those seemingly impossible dualities, in those moments I found myself making desperate wishes that my son could be healed. I would give anything, do anything, to make him better, to make him well. I would give my life—anyone's life, actually—and found myself wishing that I could negotiate some kind of trade.

What would healing look like for Ronan? Was it already taking place in some way that extended beyond the powers of imagination and simple if ardent belief? What does it mean to "be well"? Our culture offers myriad suggestions for being "healthy," but the accompanying images (for the most part) are ones we always see: thin, young, lacking a visible disability, white. Does being healthy mean looking like a buff, blond cheerleader? How is wellness different from health? Who decides what healing is? What does it mean to be whole?

I thought about Michael W. Smith, a singer songwriter

popular among the evangelical Christian group to which, in junior high, I briefly belonged. I had just moved to a small town in Nebraska where all the girls had grown up together. I was friendless, needy, hopelessly nerdy, and therefore easily roped into attending weekly prayer meetings and writing daily journal entries about "how Jesus works every day in my life." Unfortunately, my entries, made faithfully, were not well received.

Our leader, a youth pastor named Jeremy, was a bespectacled, balding man in his early thirties who preached to his captive audience of fourteen-year-old girls teetering on the edge of puberty about why it was important to abstain from sex "until one is married," and why *The Simpsons* was an evil television show to be avoided no matter what, "even if it makes one look uncool." In one of our "private growth meetings," a description that still makes no sense to me (what were we expected to grow out of or into?), which consisted of Jeremy's asking me questions about my faith ("Do you notice our Lord and Savior moving in your heart each and every day, and do you thank him?") and my responding with what I thought were the appropriate answers ("yes" and "yes"), he flipped through my journal and sighed. "They're not supposed to be stories, Emily. They're supposed to be prayers. There's a difference." Oh.

I was no good at prayer, it seemed, in written form or otherwise. The prayer circles, when we girls stood huddled together, swinging our arms and chanting—*Jesus, I just hope that you'll just heal us and just please please please make us whole and free us from sin and make us pure. Oh, Jesus, please just take pity on us, we sinners, for all of our trespasses*—put me on the edge of giggles and I could not keep my eyes closed as instructed by our "leader," a droopy-faced girl with bleached hair and a pair of shoes to match each of her neon-colored outfits. I felt vaguely embarrassed by these emotional outpourings. Couldn't we just sit down and pray quietly like Lutherans? But no, these upstart Christians were not the demure churchgoers of my early childhood; they were *evangelicals*, a new word to me, and I wanted friends, no matter how they referred to themselves. So I wrote in the journal and I swung my arms and asked to be saved and earnestly scrunched up my face with the others. During this period I also attended Christian rock concerts, even though the melodies were horrendous and the lyrics even worse.

Michael W. sang a song about a girl called Emily, a schmaltzy, cloying song. *You're an angel waiting for wings* (meaningful pause), *Em-il-y.* During the song the girl sitting next to me (Ashley? Katie?) turned to me and said, "This song is about you, Emily." Her eyes were shining.

"Uh, that's my name," I said, shifting in my bleacher seat.

She put her hand on my knee. Her white beaded "promise bracelet" that indicated her commitment to wait until marriage to have sex dug into my thigh. "Someday you'll go to heaven and be healed, and then you won't be crippled anymore." I imagined myself as a celestial supermodel, all arms and heavily mascaraed eyes and flowing hair, strutting down some heavenly cloud-strewn catwalk. And then I really did laugh, so hard that it looked as if I were crying, and she put her arm around me and we rocked from side to side.

"I know, I know," she cooed, and we swayed together for the rest of the song as she softly muttered, "Heal us, Jesus, help us Jesus, save us, Savior, please."

Years later, I was still stumped. Did being healed mean being made to look "normal," in the sense that I'd have my leg back and look a particular way? I found the image of myself equipped with two "real" legs, running around in heaven doing who knows what, patently ridiculous. Wasn't heaven about transcendence? Wasn't the physical body rendered useless or unnecessary because it was just a vessel for the soul inside, which was the thing that actually needed saving? This was how I'd been taught to interpret the biblical passage where Jesus appears at the empty tomb and instructs his grieving visitors not to worry. He was fine! His soul was up in heaven with the Father and he was beyond all bodily concerns, the horrors of the crucifixion already a dim memory. I imagined myself as a kind of holy phantom rushing around like wind in the clouds, my soul united with all the other souls that had gone to the right place, all of us bodiless and free. This was my picture of heaven as a child, and now I felt confused and wanted to talk about it.

I asked our youth director about this issue at one of our "growth" meetings. He blinked at me. "Heaven is the resurrection," he stated firmly.

"With or without the body?" I asked, because I was ready to chuck mine. I could have debated this issue with my pastor father, but I was a teenager and therefore convinced that he knew absolutely nothing about anything.

"It's a resurrection," he repeated. "It means you'll be perfect."

"You mean normal?"

He blushed. "Yes, that's right," he said finally. He handed my journal back to me. "You'll be perfectly normal. Now, isn't that something to look forward to?" Resurrection=Perfection? Sure.

Flash forward sixteen years. I was a writer-in-residence at a college in rural Pennsylvania. On this particular autumn afternoon I was sitting in a living room with a group of divorcées ranging in age from thirty to sixty-five and learning to practice the healing art of Reiki, level one. Reiki is a system of energy healing that involves the laying on of hands at certain points (face, chest, shoulders, et cetera) on the patient's body. The practitioner's palms channel healing energy to the patient that, far from being prescriptive, has no predetermined end point but is meant simply to serve that person's "highest good." Several months before, I'd seen an ad for a Reiki healer in the local grocery store, figured I could use some healing and became instantly addicted. After weekly treatments I left my practitioner's small house perched at the end of a gravel road feeling electric, euphoric and weirdly complete.

"I can feel your whole left leg," my practitioner would say, and I believed her. "It gives off its own energy, even though it's not there."

"Like a phantom limb?" I asked.

She nodded. "Only without the pain attached. No throbbing or heat. Is it throbbing?" It was not. No wonder I felt so fantastic.

During our first training session, the Reiki master, a tall blond woman from upstate New York, was educating us about the Reiki notion of wholeness. "See this," she said, pointing to the image of a torn leaf. Where the other half of the leaf had broken off she carefully drew a dotted line. "In Reiki, everything is whole, or at least holds the whole within itself. In other words, all of you are already perfect." A few women started to cry.

I raised my hand. "So healing could mean something unexpected. I mean, it wouldn't necessarily look the way we think it should." A small water fountain trickled in the corner of the room. Red and gold leaves fell past the window outside. I tried to imagine myself as an uncrippled angel, spiriting across the lawn.

The master nodded. "The idea isn't about achieving wholeness, but about what the body of that person needs, and this wisdom is housed exclusively within the body itself."

"What about curing things, such as ailments or pain, or what about cancer?" one woman asked.

Our master motioned one of the students over to the table and asked her to lie down. "Reiki energy doesn't save people in the way we've come to understand it according to Western medical practices," our teacher cautioned. "It simply helps the body do what it needs to do." In the case of her father-in-law, who'd had stage 4 cancer, the healing energy allowed him to die peacefully in his home. "I treated him every day," she said, "until the very end. Dying was what his body needed to do."

"So it helps with hospice care?" one woman asked, her voice trembling. She had just been left by her husband of thirty-seven years for a twentysomething massage therapist and now her mother was dying. She was learning Reiki to try to ease her mother's passage when all conventional methods of comfort had failed. The master hovered over the woman on the table, inhaled and placed her palms on her shoulders. "That's exactly right," she said. The woman who had asked the question began to weep quietly.

The Reiki method of healing trusts the body to give itself what it needs with the practitioner's help, and the healing is directed to moment-by-moment experience, not to an end goal. There's an instructive parallel here in terms of writing, which has the cathartic power of a therapeutic practice but lacks the ultimate goal of traditional therapy: wellness, emotional regulation. As I drove home from those Reiki treatments down the rain-soaked rural Pennsylvania roads, I felt calm, complete and content. Vibrant yet settled. A kind of healing, then, but not one that involved a dramatic physical transformation or the sudden adoption of a new body. A new leg did not miraculously sprout forth to help me start running heavenly marathons. It was much more complicated and interesting than that.

When I treated the woman whose mother was dying, I felt

the change in energy as I worked on different parts of her body. Her forehead and shoulders were cool, but there was an unmistakable heat all around her heart. After the treatment she seemed relieved, and when she treated me, I also felt a great lift, a shift into a surprising but gentle equilibrium. Nothing was "fixed," but the air felt qualitatively different. The room felt charged. Could these shifts be proved diagnostically, under a microscope or in a therapy session according to some other metrics? No, probably not. But was healing taking place? I thought so.

What did this mean for Ronan? I gave my son regular Reiki treatments and massages. He saw his acupuncturist at least once a month and a physical therapist each week. In April, Ronan saw a Japanese sensei. This renowned teacher of acupuncture treated both of us in a large sunlit room that reminded me of a church fellowship hall. Lying on tables organized in careful rows were people in various stages of partial undress. Above them, hovering, touching, laboring, were three or more acupuncturists taking pulses, touching feet, inserting needles and quietly consulting about the diagnosis in urgent whispers.

A crowd of people gathered around Ronan. He squawked, loving the attention (he inherited more than just the Tay-Sachs gene from me). Tiny tools that resembled metal toothpicks were used to stimulate points in his chubby knees and along his stomach and back. Ronan played with a colorful blue and gold pillow as the sensei scraped his meridians and diagnosed him: a weak spleen. But, he said, "he tells me he's happy." Ronan answered this pronouncement with a happy shriek. "Gee, gee, gee," he chattered, making conversation.

When it came time for my treatment, three different pairs of hands massaged and needled and diagnosed. "She's strong but fragile," I heard someone say. "Here, work on this meridian." When there was a change sensed in the body, the diagnosis changed and the strategy shifted. Each moment was taken individually. The end goal? To enable the body to do what it needed to do, whatever that might be, in that particular moment. In other words, no breaking free of the leg braces à la Forrest Gump, no miraculous healing of a disease that in turn suggested an open landscape free of pain, a future that was fixed and without struggle.

In both Reiki and acupuncture, there is no effort to make anyone "whole" or "better" in the way my friend at the Christian rock concert had understood it. My youth pastor led me to believe that my real life, my perfect life, would begin after my death, and that what I did on earth was merely a preparatory journey for that final transformation. I thought about the call and response during Easter Sunday services: "He is risen!" "He is risen indeed!" For Reiki masters and acupuncturists of many different lineages, the goal is comfort in the moment, now, here, in your body. The second approach, especially in light of my experience of parenting Ronan, made a lot more sense.

Along the high road to Taos from Santa Fe is a village called Chimayó, famous for its "sanctuario" of healing dirt and for the annual Easter pilgrimage when long lines of faithful penitents armed with electric torches and wearing illuminated clothing traipse to the church along I-25. Some of them travel the last few feet on their hands and knees. I'd been to Chimayó at least five times since moving to Santa Fe, but only once in the winter. In a quiet back room of the main church, a small hole in the ground is full of soft, dark dirt that is cool to the touch, like slightly damp sand. A handwritten sign on the wall tells you that if you have a handicap (check) and a broken heart (check), you will find solace there. I didn't believe this, not really, but I always found myself scooping up a bit of the dirt and rubbing it on Ronan; sometimes I would eat a fingerful of it. I bought a silver vial that I filled with dirt and wore around my neck on a black silk cord. I liked the mystery inherent in magical thinking, the glittering possibility, the earnest vulnerability. And what do we really know? Very little, it seems. Even Saint Paul, the thinker whom few dare to argue with, didn't believe that we were getting the whole picture of what our lives were about or might be in the future or the afterlife. We were, all of us, peering anxiously through that dark glass, desperate for a glimpse of the other side. And I did find solace in this church, perhaps because those who visit Chimayó for healing seem fueled by ardent, inconvenient beliefs, and this struggle suggested a powerful stubbornness that I appreciated and admired, as much as I could no longer subscribe to those beliefs. And although I no longer identified with the stringency or dogma of organized Christian religion, I remained drawn to the compassion and sense of community that still existed in houses of worship.

The walls of the corridor outside the room that houses the holy dirt are lined with shiny metal crutches, a few worn out, scuffed canes—all apparently abandoned after the healing dirt did its magic. The entirety of one wall is papered with photographs of servicemen and -women who have died in the last ten years in various wars, the bulk of them between nineteen and twenty-three years old. The place is thronged with people during the summer months, but during the late winter and early spring there are fewer pilgrims, no bustle of bodies or rosaries being slipped through the fingers of tourists at the Vigil Store, where I often picked up a medallion or a small painted *retablo* for Ronan's room. On my last winter visit it seemed that nobody was keeping vigil at all. The churches were bone cold, the pews empty. There was a man sawing a piece of wood in one of the side chapels where an elaborately dressed doll, wearing blue and white fluttery skirts—the Madonna—stood collecting dust behind a pane of recently cleaned glass. A sign advertising espresso drinks in a side street café creaked back and forth in the wind. In the children's chapel, the back room was stacked wall to wall with baby shoes for Santo Niño de Atocha, the child Jesus, and a woman was singing "The Old Rugged Cross" as she swept the wooden floors. I love the religious folk art, the red and blue wooden birds swinging from the ceilings, the sky-blue birds perched at the baptismal font and the random stray dogs that will wander in and lick a baby's hand if you sit in the pews long enough. I love the old confessional booth with the place for the penitent to kneel *outside*, where everyone would hear your transgressions and listen as you asked for and were granted forgiveness. Near the door are a few children's graves that I'd never noticed before. The entrance gate is guarded by a colorful symbol of Santo Niño himself, all cherubic with golden curls and red and yellow robes. I went to Chimayó because a secret but eager part of me wanted to believe in healing as a magic trick, physical salvation at the flick of a sanctified wrist, dirt placed on the affected part accomplishing a stunning, instantaneous change. I wanted someone to say, as Jesus did to a man's dead daughter in the Gospels, "Child! Get up!" I knew it would not happen. But something else might.

After Ronan was diagnosed I began to question understandings of what healing meant, what it symbolized, how it was done. I reread Simone Weil, a thinker who understands healing as a psychological process, one that demands obedience and waiting. The twisting, labyrinthine world is full of chance, secret places, uncontrollable chaos and unknown roads that, if we wait long enough, might be explained or revealed, or they might never be. As she says in *Forms of the Implicit Love of God:* "The beauty of the world is the mouth of a labyrinth."

I found comfort in Weil's notion of waiting for God, not as a passive action but as a patient practice, one that required concentration as well as stillness and a hope that refused to fixate on a particular predetermined outcome. I thought about the biblical narratives where Jesus heals the sick with a brush of his cloak, makes the unclean clean, casts out demons, and makes the lame walk, the blind see, the barren fertile, and so forth. In any case, the body is a problem to be solved and Jesus can solve it.

Healing, for Ronan, would not mean the radical healing of his physical form. It might mean instead his full acceptance into community, into family, not the fixing of his physical body. Healing might mean no prayers for a miracle but prayers for his peaceful, albeit short, life. Healing might mean waiting, as Simone Weil did, for God to *arrive*, to fall into the person, and she offered no predetermined notions of what that might look or be like or feel like. Healing for Ronan might simply mean people meeting him and experiencing his uniqueness without thinking *He's blind, he's paralyzed, he's deaf, he's retarded* when he was all of these things. As Becky, another dragon mom, pointed out to me, our minds are littered with these classifications that block us from seeing the beauty of individual souls housed in particular bodies.

After my level-one Reiki training there was a kind of initiation that can only be described as a benediction, but instead of the pastor's hands rising at the end of the service to send us out in the world, my eyes were closed. I felt the master's hands sweeping and swooping through the air above my head, commanding me to use this energy for good alone. She asked me to heal others and myself (all Reiki practitioners can heal themselves). I would not be resurrected or reawakened into glossy, rosy-cheeked perfection, galloping through heaven on two flesh-and-blood legs. I was right to view that visualization of healing or wholeness as misguided. The potential of Ronan to heal and be healed had little to do with his body and more to do with how he was accepted in the larger world. That, perhaps, was the healing task, and if it happened universally, everywhere we went, it would indeed feel like a miracle.

Until I encountered Reiki and acupuncture, I had understood healing in a narrow, prescriptive way, as an end point predicated on the assumption that there is something deeply wrong with the person being healed, otherwise why bother? But the philosophies that undergird Reiki and acupuncture understand the body as an inherently wise vessel having a unique and valuable experience that can be made more comfortable and wonderful through the treatments these systems of thought have generated and provide. My son's body would not be healed. Tay-Sachs disease, described accurately, I believe, as a demon, would not be "cast out." His healing experiences would never add up to "healing" the way I had previously understood it. If Jesus were alive and I jostled up to him in a crowd with Ronan in my arms and touched his cloak, I would not suddenly grow a new leg, and Ronan would not start walking and talking and holding his head up without assistance. But as a result of the teachings of Jesus, people might regard Ronan and me differently, and with respect: the outcasts, the outsiders, brought into the communal fold. Having answered the question "What's wrong with you?" for much of my life, I could scarcely imagine such acceptance, but I wished it for my son, and although I could not heal him, I could insist that he be accepted for who and how he was.

Ronan lived in the world held by people who loved him and fed him and talked with him and met him on his own terms. When he died, he will have been fully loved from his first breath to his last and then after. That full uncompromising love, powerful and sometimes painful, was perhaps the only miracle worth believing in.

14

Spring arrived, although little felt new or promising to me. I found myself uninterested in all the warm weather anticipation, although I couldn't help but notice a few trees beginning to bloom, flashes of green and white and pink appearing along the arroyo path. I wanted to spirit Ronan away to a cave on some windswept cliff with a view of the ocean where we could live with only the sounds of sea animals and unpredictable waves to keep us company. Ronan and I living on the coast of Donegal in the north of Ireland. Cold, damp Irish weather that smelled of wet wool and hot milk tea. A gray, complicated sky. It sounded like heaven, or at the very least a different place to be, which was why the concept of heaven appears to have been invented in the first place.

I distrusted all the supposed thrill of newness, the sunshine and bright light of spring, all the old certainties promised by

the season (renewal, resurrection, salvation). I was simply waiting for and anticipating an end; I grieved a little bit at a time,
each day a little bit more, and then this and then that, day after
day after day. Where was the relief in all that dread? As usual,
in unexpected places.

On a blustery April afternoon, Ronan, Rick and I visited
the Kindred Spirits Animal Sanctuary, a hospice care facility
for animals. This haven, a wide swath of ranch land in the
middle of a wind-swept desert, is owned and operated by Ulla
Pedersen, a Danish native who has been providing end-of-life
care for dogs, horses and poultry for more than two decades.
We parked near the white ranch gate at the end of a gravel road
south of Santa Fe. It was, as Ulla noted, a "blowy" day, and the
dry hills in the distance seemed covered in a veil of sand. Ulla,
short and strong and with flashing blue eyes, explained that
because she grew up on a farm in Denmark, animals were always an essential part of her life. I wanted to bring Ronan to
the sanctuary because we had no household pets, and I'd always
considered my own experiences with animals, particularly with
dogs, to be some of the most profound of my life.

First we met Bo, a thirty-year-old horse who had been se-
verely abused and suffered from Cushing's disease. With his
dark head and a white diamond on his nose, a swayed back and
blurry eyes, he looked like an unfortunate creature in a children's story. Ulla fed him part of a carrot from her palm. Bo
sniffed Ronan's head and seemed uninterested. In the corral
behind the two stalls spread with fresh straw another horse

wandered, Bo's friend Toki, also thirty. "Horses attract abusers," Ulla explained. "It's about power." I didn't push for additional details. Both horses had been with her for more than two decades.

A pack of four dogs approached us—a few blind, some with gray-sprinkled muzzles and all with arthritic back legs, others with bits of gray on their noses that looked like accidents of paint, or flags of age waiting to flutter farther up their faces. They followed us, limping and sniffing us and then trotting along beside us as we walked to the poultry area. These were just four of the twenty-two dogs currently living at Kindred Spirits, all of them previously abandoned or abused, some of them, according to Ulla, "because they got a little bit old and the owners couldn't deal with it." Others had been kicked or burned or left on the side of the road. The sanctuary received "Can you take my old dog?" calls every day.

During their first days on the ranch the dogs were often skittish and fearful and terribly sleepy, but eventually, Ulla noted, they felt safe and at home, and their personalities bloomed. "Some are only with us a short time," she said, "but we know that those final days are good ones."

Dogs were treated to acupuncture, "brush and cuddle" treatments from volunteers and organic food. Very few drugs were used, although the dogs suffered ailments ranging from a hanging jaw, blindness, severe arthritis, back and leg issues, and other complications of old age. Each dog "tells" Ulla his or her name, and so Lil Bit Buddha and Anna-Lisa and Oscar and

Abuelita and many others wandered a yard full of communal dog beds, ragged hairy blankets and saggy old mattresses: a dog's paradise, full of dirt and stink and color. Buddhist prayer flags waved from posts and clotheslines. Just outside the entrance to the chicken coop was the memorial shrine for Salvador. A photograph of his golden, smiling face was propped up against a tree, his collar swinging from one of the sturdier branches. Someone had left a few bones for him. I thought of my own various shrines to my dead St. Bernard, Bandit. A framed sketch of him hung on the wall over Ronan's changing table; another hung on the kitchen wall. An enormous photograph of him looking regal and serene on a beach in Provincetown was placed just above my writing desk; his collar and paw prints were preserved in a glass-covered box, also mounted on the wall of the study.

From each dog's collar hung a silver medallion with Saint Francis on one side and Saint Anthony on the other. In the "big dog" room there were bunk beds and dog beds, while the smaller dogs shared recliners and small love seats. Statues of Buddha or Saint Francis peeked out from beneath scraggly bushes. The ranch was peaceful, if windblown, with barks, whinnies and a riot of quacks ringing through the air at intervals as regular as church bells marking time. Ronan whined a little, and cooed a bit when Rick bent down with him and let the dogs lick his fingers.

In the first poultry room, old ducks splashed in the mud and roosters and hens gathered in various "neighborhoods":

cozy spaces and nests under boxes and other wooden structures. Some of the birds had been found along the side of New Mexico roads in various states of distress; some were found in trash cans. Their sleeping room was lined with photos of chickens, as if birds, too, longed for pinups on their bedroom walls. In the second poultry room, protected from birds of prey by a wire "ceiling" over the area, an eighteen-year-old turkey, like something out of a Thanksgiving pageant, strutted around in his black-and-white speckled glory. "If people are going to eat them, they should see them first," Ulla said. Two regal peacocks were swanning around the volunteer-made wetlands ("Mud is good for birds," Ulla explained), leaving behind a trail of delicate, tendrillike green feathers, each with a blue center that reminded me of the "evil eye" medallions I'd once seen for sale in the shops of Greece, talismans meant to ward off bad luck. "When they are molting, the yard is covered in feathers," Ulla told us, and I imagined the ground swarming with inky blue eyes, ground that was thick with good fortune. The peacock made a sharp, shrill sound—part cat, part bird—his pointed beak opening only slightly. I rescued a stray feather and stroked Ronan's face with it. The day before I had taken him for a hike on the Borrego Trail, waved a pine needle underneath his nose and brushed his bare chubby feet over the dirt.

Inside the house, volunteers cooked meals and cleaned beds. A small Chihuahua with deformed feet—she was saved from a puppy mill—let us know with a few sharp barks that this was her territory. Ulla led us to the back room, which, in addition to housing the sanctuary's newest addition, was lined with memorials and remembrances of each and every animal that had ever lived at the sanctuary. Tiny paw print frames, photos, favorite toys, poems, paintings. "It's very, very important that each animal be remembered," Ulla said, and her gentle voice and unassuming manner—this grand but unsentimental acceptance of the good and the bad together—made me believe that she'd been an excellent bereavement counselor, work she had done for many years.

So much has been written about the connections between animals and humans, but before I had Ronan, even though I loved my old dog Bandit fiercely through his various unknown ailments, bladder infections, tumors, incontinence, worms (hook and heart), eye infections and expensive, late-night vet appointments, I never fully understood this deep connection. In some ways, much of Ronan's experience was at the animal level: immediate touch, taste, sight, sound with no cognitive recall; there was no storing of memories, joyful or fearful or terrifying or liberating or otherwise. Just bald experience that ended as quickly as it began: a feather brushed against a cheek, a startling sound, the surprise of a new sensation, and then it's forgotten. Ronan sat on the mattress with Anna-Lisa; Abuelita, trembling with fear, was still brave enough to lick his hand with her tiny red poodle tongue. A rooster fluttered past Ronan's face, his comb a band of color briefly crossing Ronan's vision. And then? Forgotten. Only I remembered, a necessary if sometimes arduous task.

My friend Tara, years after losing her dog, her apricot beauty Theda, wrote to me when we were discussing the impossibility of loss and the mind's stubborn refusal to accept what was so terrible: "Isn't she just in the next room, right next door?" I thought of this as I looked at the tributes to all these creatures, many of them with unknown histories, but all of them with known ends. All of them loved. We don't forget after we let go. Tara was right, and both moves—the knowing of the loss and the refusal to fully know it, both of which are different from intellectual acceptance—are essential parts of love.

I asked Ulla if we could come back as Ronan's condition progressed, perhaps just to sit on the lawn and let the dogs surround him, explore, interact, and then, at night, we would leave them to sleep their animal dreams under the black dome of sky, in their eclectic pack, safe, without at all remembering Ronan, who would be in his own room, safe for the moment even as he was dying, dreaming his own unknown dreams. My baby, mine. Pablo Neruda, "Rest with your dream in my dream."

I pulled away from the sanctuary brimming with a strange, electrified feeling. A feeling of fullness, a kind of swarm in the belly, my heart beating quickly, my cheeks flushed. Driving back home I burst into tears. Looking at those shrines, touching those animal bodies, I realized that I'd been thinking, all that time, that Ronan would always be, in some way, right in the other room, in the next room, in every room. Wouldn't he?

15

The blazing evidence of immortality is our
dissatisfaction with any other solution.

—Ralph Waldo Emerson

On a warm afternoon in April, I found myself kneeling in
the garage, sorting through a black garbage bag stuffed
with Ronan's outgrown baby clothes. I had promised to give
them away to a friend who had a friend who knew a friend who
was raising a little boy on her own. I wanted to do this good
deed; it made me feel good to think about trotting off to the
post office with a taped-up box full of clothes for this woman
I'd never meet, a boy I'd never know. But as I sorted through the
onesies printed with dogs and dinosaurs and stars; a green onesie with "Organic Baby" printed over the outline of a leaf; a
cream-colored onesie with "I Am a Magical Child" printed in
cursive over a picture of a unicorn and a dragon; tie-dyed onesies with matching hats and missing socks; hand-me-down one-

sies; bear and lion and other jungle-animal onesies; jean jackets and OshKosh overalls and corduroy jeans and cargo pants (what does a baby do with pockets?); shirts that said "Doggone Fun" and "Surfer Baby" and "Handsome Like Daddy" and "There's a Nap in my Future"; a pale yellow cotton one-piece with a collar and a fire engine stitched on with a door that actually opens and closes, real snaps at the neck, even a little fabric flap for the firehouse dog that wore a red hat (this last outfit belonged to my brother Andy), I closed the plastic bag and wept.

The weight of these things was too much. I felt as though I had just peered into the deep pit of a grave. I could picture Ronan in every little outgrown outfit: the skinny-legged, newly born, red-faced alien Ronan; the round bowling-ball face of five- and then six-month Ronan; the one-year-old Ronan with the light already fading, just a bit, from his eyes. The floppy toddler Ronan who was now double the size of these clothes and dying fast. I could not give them away. Not yet. I wanted them for myself, and I wanted back that innocent time when I thought I would watch my son grow up. I wanted to get in the bag and eat the clothes like some starving animal, some desperate creature. I scolded myself: *these are just things, nothing more.* Just objects, and, even more important, items other people needed. I still couldn't do it. I closed up the bags and went inside. I thought of these lines from a 1913 letter by Marcel Proust: *We think we do not love our dead but that is because we do not remember them: suddenly we catch sight of an old glove and burst into tears.*

I suppose this was a sentimental moment. On a sympathy

card there might be a bunny, or a lovely sunset, or the dark silhouette of a bird flying over a beach, a shiny horse running free, a hawk doing something symbolic. I didn't like this moment with the clothes any more than I like sympathy cards or funerals, which so easily and lustily dip into sentimentality. I felt dangerous and churning because sentimentality masks a deep and terrible rage. Bunnies = rage. The murderous kind, the bite-your-lip-until-it-bleeds kind, the exhausting-but-too-manic-to-sleep kind. The only appropriate card for this moment, on my knees in the garage, was an empty one, maybe one that screams when you open it—one great, long keen. Some deep-noted dirge; some furious, melancholic song full of discord and drums. The responses I found most satisfying—like a bell ringing out the hour—after Ronan's diagnosis were these: *I am so fucking angry; I am thinking of you with grief and rage; I don't even know what to say I am so super fucking angry; it is so fucking unfair; I am sick to my stomach with sadness and anger; BLOODY UN-FAIR!, I LOVE YOU and also WHAT THE FUCK? RAGE!*

Sympathy cards are about as useless as candy cigarettes—just give me the real thing. I'd so much rather have an e-mail that says something brutal and terrible and true than a sympathy card that's made of soft-to-the-touch-parchment, the edges gently serrated, decorated with loathsome, uniform birds (there is a sympathy card bird; it's like clip art) flying peacefully into the distance and a super shitty rhyming poem inside. (I do not even dare type them here for fear of expanding their odious reach.)

On my knees in the garage I wanted this poem: "Matins,"
by Louise Gluck:

> You want to know how I spend my time?
> I walk the front lawn, pretending
> to be weeding. You ought to know
> I'm never weeding, on my knees, pulling
> clumps of clover from the flower beds: in fact
> I'm looking for courage, for some evidence
> my life will change, though
> it takes forever, checking
> each clump for the symbolic
> leaf, and soon the summer is ending, already
> the leaves are turning, always the sick trees
> going first, the dying turning
> brilliant yellow, while a few dark birds perform
> their curfew of music. You want to see my hands?
> As empty now as at the first note.
> Or was the point always
> to continue without a sign?

Why didn't that poem, that little missile of grief, come
printed in a card? I'd happily weep over it or frame it or burn
it up in some meaningful ritual fire. When I opened the pastel
envelopes and saw the birds and the sunsets and the birds
scrolling into the gentle sunset, cards sent for Ronan, for me, I
chucked them straight away. I didn't even look to see who sent

them and I didn't care if this was cruel. "They're trying to be nice," my mom told me. I did not care. The era of being nice was over.

Would I feel so unaccountably devastated about giving away outgrown baby clothes if Ronan were not dying? I knew plenty of moms who had blubbered as they sorted through baby clothes, even if their child was a teenager, sulking grumpily in his man cave and playing video games and trying to watch porn or smoke pot when his parents weren't paying attention. And yes, they were just clothes, but just as the body carries physical and psychic weight, so do things: a favorite shirt of the beloved, obvious objects like wedding rings, but also random things given and received: a map my best friend Emily made for me ten years ago showing me the way from the train station to her house in South London; the lyrics of a song written on a napkin that I sang at her wedding; my "Duke" sweatshirt that I stole from someone's brother in high school and wore superstitiously for four years during finals in college; a creamy flowered blouse that reminded me of France and a steamy night spent making out in a Strasbourg car park with that blouse in a pretty ball on the floor of my date's Peugeot. Mini menorahs and cigarette holders were found in the corners of tenements and are on display now under glass at the Tenement Museum in New York City, precious items that were tucked into underwear or satchels or shoes and that crossed continents and made it through the gauntlet of checkers at Ellis Island (early, less technologically advanced versions of today's snarky TSA agents) to be found, decades later, abandoned, in a corner. And things mattered more then, too, because people had fewer of them.

Things are charged, hierophanic; we believe, often unconsciously, that they act as gateways to the person who once inhabited them, that they are doors to worlds, portals to stories we intuit even if we don't know the narrative for certain or for sure. I have a cheap dress—blue polyester with red and white piping on the bottom and the sleeves—that puts me chain-smoking in Geneva on a blazing hot spring morning, the view across the garden thick with pink blossoms. My Dr. Martens boots were my Ireland boots, trekking boots; I literally wore them out—after one year the soles were finished. When my mom was given her mother's old cameo necklace from a cousin, she said "Oh," almost mutely, amazed, her eyes filling as she turned the necklace over in her hands like a piece of delicate lace. I saw her seeing it on her mother's throat, her mother who had been dead for forty years and had been given this piece of jewelry, now falling apart, by an old boyfriend who was not my mother's father, who was also dead. Things matter, things endure when people and relationships do not. *Things: simply lasting, then / failing to last: water, a blue heron's / eye, and the light passing / between them: into light all things / must fall, glad at last to have fallen.* (Jane Kenyon's "Things")

Things, things, things. I have always been a collector of things. A windy Wyoming storage room packed floor to ceiling with books, a box full of artificial legs, old cotton cloth Esprit bags full of scattered photos from junior high, me sitting in clumps of girls at pizza parties and sleepovers, sticking out my chest in an effort to look busty and gregarious. (I was flat-chested and miserable.) At least ten jewelry boxes stuffed with cheap and ruined jewelry, rhinestones and crystals and rusty charms shaped like tigers and elephants. Boxes of letters and three boxes of all the cards I got as a kid when I was in the hospital. A box of prom dresses and bridesmaids' dresses, more boxes full of journals and math workbooks and yearbooks and notes that I passed and that were passed to me in junior high and high school. Someday, when my parents move out of their house and clean out their basement for good, I'll have to reckon with my pack-rat self. But not yet.

After Ronan's diagnosis I began collecting things for Ronan and arranging them on what I called "the magic shelf," just above his crib. A shrine box, a tiny unicorn ornament, a statue of Saint Anthony with a child on his hip, a friend's sister's rosary, wooden train cars that spell RONAN in red and blue and green, a pocket-sized Buddha statue, rocks and seashells from Provincetown and Maine, Day of the Dead figurines. I tried to carry the magic with me as well: around my neck a silk cord swinging with my box of holy dirt from Chimayó, my Buddha, my Santa Niño charm. Tucked in the drawer of my bedside table was a Ziploc bag full of Ronan's hair—tiny red-gold curls and wisps—from his first haircut. After Ronan died I imagined gathering up the contents of his magic shelf into a bag that I could wear around my neck or my waist and tear and claw at, like a homemade garment of mourning.

Things matter, things count. The Swiss sweep the homes of their citizens each year and count bullets to be sure the weapons haven't been fired by any members of the peaceful, civilian army; the neutral moderators of the neutral army take out the neutral bullets and hold the neutral bits of steel in their clean, neutral hands. In 1994 a piece of a Viking ship was found near my apartment building in Dublin, which meant one less crane would be obscuring the skyline as the archaeologists arrived with their books and enthusiasm, their shovels and special tools. There's a pool of dark, cool water in a well in Dublin Castle that has been sitting there since AD years were in the single digits. In one legendary story, Mary Shelley kept her husband's dehydrated heart—then just a handful of powdery dust— inside a copy of one of his poems. In Victorian times you didn't send a letter to your beloved through the post, you sent a lock of your snipped hair, like a pressed flower or a leaf plucked from a tree. Things make people—and memories—accessible, digestible, permanent feeling, like some kind of marking, like a portable, off-body tattoo.

Things. We adorn, we bedeck, we festoon. We search and select gifts for our beloved. *I saw this and thought of you.* A ring from Paris, a scarf from Wisconsin, a hand-knit sweater with your name on a tag stitched inside, a tattoo sleeve stretching from shoulder to wrist. A clutch of coins from countries you've visited, currency that's useless in your own country that you can chuck into a big plastic bin for charity in airports in Madrid, London, Berlin. Marks, shekels, pounds, euros, francs, pence, lire, Canadian dollars.

When I saw a mother walking on the arroyo path in Santa Fe with a baby in the front pack, I thought, *She's what, maybe eleven pounds*? I guessed that the premature nine-month-old twin girl in Ronan's swimming class weighed about seven pounds. The woman who sat next to me during a turbulent plane ride in the 1990s, back when flying absolutely terrified me, said, "It's virtually impossible for these planes to fall out of the sky. They weigh too much to fall." (Too big to fail!) An artificial leg weighs between ten or fifteen pounds; an artificial foot weighs about four or five; the "model" legs (like model homes) that are lined up along the walls of a prosthetist's office are often lighter, the ones that hang from straps and pulleys in the back rooms, the ones for real people, are the weight they should be and of course these weights range—they are as individual as the people who wear them. When I was eighteen, I weighed 95 pounds; when I was breast-feeding Ronan, I weighed 110 pounds; in Geneva I weighed 132 pounds. Ronan weighed 6.5 pounds when he was born, and doubled his weight within the first three weeks of life. At eighteen months he weighed 24 pounds and I weighed 116 pounds. A bag of outgrown baby clothes weighs 5.4 pounds. Grief weighs nothing, but you still have to drag it around.

Ronan, where are you going? Literally beyond me. *Will I see you again? When did you begin?* Was I asleep in the Brentwood studio, late-night traffic still a low and steady hum a few blocks away on Wilshire Boulevard, the ocean sloshing back and forth against the beach less than a mile away? Was I writing at the Novel Café in Venice, California, batting flies away from my *huevos salsa verde? Oh, where are you going?* Will I be walking down the street someday and recognize your multicolored, thick-lashed eyes in the pale face of another little boy? Will I catch the edge of your mellow sweetness in a neighbor's dog that nuzzles my hand in the street? If science tells us that energy never stops completely but is endlessly recycled, does this mean that Buddhist notions about reincarnation and the transmigration of souls have some truth to them and that death is just a gateway to a new experience? Or is energy tightly packed up in the Christian heaven, itself a kind of holy clearinghouse for souls or energy bodies roaming free, released from the bonds of physical impediment? Both concepts require that some element of that person is sustained, endlessly protected, and in some sense living on—the essence, the soul, something. And I also thought about karma, this notion that each of us must live out old stories that are unknown to or at least well hidden from us in this current existence, which seemed both unfair as well as an inadequate way of explaining the unfairness of life.

Overwhelmed by notions of karma, I wandered to the bookcase and thought *Poets! Help me!* I found this poem by my friend Phil Pardi, itself from a book of meditations:

DRINKING WITH MY FATHER IN LONDON

With his mate, Wilfred, who was dying
I discussed ornithology as best I could
Given the circumstances, my father flushed
And silent, a second pint before me,
My fish and chips not yet in sight.
Condensation covered the windows
and in the corner a couple played
tic-tac-toe with their fingers.
Behind it all, convincingly, the rain fell.
The mystery, Wilfred was saying, *isn't flight.*
Flight is easy, he says, lifting his cap, *but*
landing—he tosses it at the coat rack—
landing is the miracle. Would you believe
thirty feet away the cap hits
and softly takes in the one bare peg?
Would you believe no one but me notices?
I'd like to come back as a bird,
Wilfred says, both hands on the glass
before him, and here my father
comes to life. *You already*
were a bird once,
Wilfred, he says, *next time*
next time you get to be
the whole damn flock.

What did I believe? I believed that I was sad, and would always be sad. Beyond that, who knew? My belief was short-sighted and myopic, as most beliefs are.

"Terror breeds apocalyptic visions," a religion professor once told me when we were discussing the origins of the Book of Revelation. No shit. It is impossible to believe in the unbeliev-able just to find a way of moving through a difficult experience— or even just a single day. But I've always believed in the power of stories to make life cohere, to create a necessary order around us, and this can, in turn, help us fully live. And all of the no-tions of the afterlife are, of course, stories. People may ardently believe in them, as incredulous as they are to nonbelievers, but the truth is that nobody has come back to verify the facts of anybody's vision of the afterlife. No empirical evidence exists. Nobody knows anything for sure. Not Saint Paul, not the ear-liest translators of the Bible, not the redactors of the Bible itself, not even Jesus, who did most of his talking about the afterlife and what it meant and how we would get there before he died. What happened to him afterward, in that beyond, is purely con-jecture. We can only believe in what we've come to accept as truth. No abstract notions of morality can effectively guide us. We only have stories. In the song "Guided by Wire," Neko Case sings: *The voices that did comfort me are furthest from my sanity / Have come from places I have never seen / Even in my darkest recollection / There was someone singing my life back to me.* In my friend Barbara's letter from around this time she reminded me of the scene in one of Philip

Pullman's novels when Lyra must tell stories in order to set the trapped souls free, and how the experience nearly kills her. In Buddhism we're invited to see ourselves as part of the natural cycle of birth, aging and dying. Stories: they're all we've got.

But all the old stories failed me. (I thought of the hymn "The Old, Old Story": *I love to tell the story / 'twill be my theme in glory / to tell the old, old story / of Jesus and his love.*) Belief in anything seemed impossible. One morning I woke up while it was still dark outside, misread my alarm clock, and found myself convinced that the sun was not going to rise. It was three in the afternoon, the world was ending, and I felt completely relieved. My private apocalypse had finally spilled over into the larger world. I wouldn't have to explain a single element of my personal tragedy. Everyone else would be having one as well. *Bad karma,* I heard a voice inside of me say. *You've got to give love to get love!*

The notion of karma troubled me because it felt like something real to hook into and wasn't attached to a unique, gendered deity to whom I was supposed to feel indebted for my life. It felt the most true and yet it was the most problematic because it seemed the most closely linked to retribution, to punishment, even if it was not inflicted by a god or a godlike being.

Many of the healers and Buddhists and others I spoke to after Ronan's diagnosis tried to soft-pedal karma, but they all insisted that we benefit and suffer from karmic motion. My initial reaction to the idea that Ronan's karmic fate was the reason he would live for only a few years, after regressing into a vegetative state, was to look at his chubby baby face and chubby baby thighs and feel angry and helpless. How ludicrous. Why give such a load to a baby? Why dump it on a baby's parents?

If the vague karmic inferences angered me, the specific Christian forecasting scared me.

In the fall before Ronan was diagnosed, I was walking with my friend Rob on the arroyo path near his house in Santa Fe when a woman passed us, curious about the baby contentedly snoozing in the front pack. After I told her Ronan's name she repeated it and asked me if I'd had him baptized yet. I said no and walked on, making light of it. We passed her again: she asked again about the baptism. *What about Ronan?* she asked. Rob told her, quite rightly, that she was being rude (he said it in the nicest way), but days after Ronan's diagnosis I found myself haunted by this question. Was that woman some kind of special seer who knew that my baby was sick long before I did and was giving me solid advice about how to help him? What *about* Ronan? Had I failed my son by not having him baptized? Had I failed to protect him somehow by not assuring his safe passage through purgatory and into heaven with all the other doomed babies? Or is baptism, as Simone Weil believed, just a big bowl of dangerous groupthink? When Rick and I took Infant Care I, the teacher was sure to remind us that *a baby can drown in just an inch of water.* Is the baptismal font full of enough water for a person—not just a baby—to drown in?

Several years ago I was walking Emily's son Coll to his school in south London. A fearless kid, he wanted to run ahead and promised to stop and wait for me at the corner before crossing the street. He assured me several times that this would be perfectly acceptable to his parents. I was pushing his sister Anita in the stroller, watching Coll's white-blond hair flapping in the wind, dust flying up from the soles of his shoes, buses and cars roaring past. Nervous, I frantically called him back to me. "If it's okay with you, I would like it if you'd walk next to me," I said, trying to mask the terror so evident on my face. (When he was just weeks old I took him for a brief walk in the stroller and didn't take one breath the entire time.) He was annoyed, but he patiently walked with us to the schoolyard, where he finally turned to me and said, "You can leave me now." I panicked. Could I? How did I know what was going to greet him on the jungle gym, in the classroom? Who can say that my protectiveness on the street meant anything at all? Being vigilant in one potentially dangerous moment was no safeguard against future trouble. Anything could happen at any time. Some wounding comment might be made and never forgotten, some maniacal swing from the monkey bars might end in a life-threatening free fall. No, I simply could not leave him at this school, where physical and emotional disaster lurked in every kid-occupied corner. I looked around for the teacher, prepared to tell her that I was taking Coll home, and trying to think of a plausible reason why this would be necessary. But before I could find a single adult he had run off, happy to be free of me, and I turned the stroller around and headed back to the house, Anita chattering along as we bumped across the park.

Em's garden faces the schoolyard of the primary school, and all afternoon I tried to comfort myself with the roar and flow of children playing beyond the wall. It's a scary word, "beyond." It looms. Like a big stretch of rocky, unseen road you are asked to navigate in the dark without shoes or a flashlight. But I heard laughter and bouncing balls. Happy shouting that was vigorous without sounding panicked. No sounds of disaster, no shrieks or gasps. I assured myself that someone would be looking out for him, that he'd be fine. Still, I was relieved when he returned home. It felt like a small miracle, and I couldn't imagine reenacting it each day. *How do parents do this?* I wondered.

How do we know when to leave people behind and when to send them off? How do we ever know where we're sending them? As a parent, I wanted to know what was waiting for my son at the end of his life; I wanted an inked scroll with an official stamp that would tell me what would happen, and I wanted to get him to the end of his short life with dignity. How will he be ushered to the other side? (*"You pressed a coin into his palm and stepped across the water"*—Dana Levin, "Styx.") I wanted to enjoy each moment he had in this life, which meant I had to learn to feel less tortured and less afraid. Otherwise, I would not be able to mother Ronan the way he deserved, and I didn't have much time to sort it out. I fed my son squash and beans and pureed pumpkin. I hiked with him in the Sangre de Cristo Mountains. I drove with him to Wyoming to see my parents. Each time we were together, doing anything, I thought: *If there is a heaven, could we do this all over again? Could all these moments repeat on an endless loop and last forever?*

Rick and I were firm about our philosophy-of-care approach: minimal intervention, maximum life experience. But when the body doesn't make the decision for us, how do we know when to leave one another? How do we know when to let go? How would I know what to do in that moment when a decision is required of me? What would be my guide? Motherly instinct, whatever that is? The harshness of scientific fact? What spoke to me in Phil's poem is the implication that any afterlife we imagine is so limited that the only thing we can do is let go of the hat and trust that it will land. We might never see it; we might be the only ones who ever do. These questions kept me awake at night, especially in the spring, with all of its false promises of renewal and birth and growth. I stood over Ronan's crib and watched him sleeping and thought, *Here he is, here he is, for now, right here.* I would stumble back to bed, try to sleep, sit up and think, as if someone had shouted in my ear: THEN WHAT?

Nobody gets a free pass. The stories I heard from some of the other Tay-Sachs parents absolutely confirmed this. Just because you watch your child die does not mean you won't shepherd your parents through a debilitating illness, or that you won't get cancer, or that your husband won't die in a car crash, or that you won't emerge a bitter and broken person. Although my great fear while I was pregnant was that they'd gotten it all wrong and my birth defect was genetic, part of me believed that I'd earned a bit of good fortune, that it was my turn to be visited by some grace. But grace is more fickle than luck; sometimes you need a magnifying glass to see it. Sometimes you need super powers. The only guide I had during my experience of parenting Ronan was imagination.

16

Living in the midst of the knowledge of Ronan's inevitable death forced me into a new kind of living. It was uncomfortable, a heavy and daily mental wade through some pretty difficult thoughts, but it was qualitatively different from the life I was living before—like a dream life, an alternative existence. It was a life of heightened presence and constant mourning, an activity of which I became a scientist. Each day I picked apart my grief with a little knife; I combed through it; I boiled it in petri dishes and tried to blow it up. I sprinkled it with gas and lit a match, watched it burn, put out the fire. It always came back, tenacious and colorful, jumping around and shouting. Each day it presented a new substance to tinker with—sticky, soft, gooey, slimy, rough. Each day it baffled. Sometimes it smiled and laughed. Managing grief was weirdly playful, the way science and art should be: experimentation, turning down new roads, taking the cue from what came before and asking always why and what if and what next? I didn't like the results of my carefully devised experiments, all of which were about ridding myself of grief and trying to simply be blazingly happy in the moments remaining with Ronan. The results of my labor were unsatisfactory. I gave myself a Big Fat F for Grief Science class, scrawled in red pen at the top of the paper. Grief is too much work; you'll never get the grade you think you deserve.

Snuggling up to my son meant snuggling up to death, I'd think, listening to "Ronan Radio" on the baby monitor and begging Xanax to provide some relief. Death—that "serial killer," as the poet Dana Levin calls it and that we all pretend we can avoid, outsex, outlove, outachieve, work out, cast off, deny deny deny. Ronan's body was already lost and yet we clung to him. What dreams did he dream in that fizzing, intricate brain that was ticking down each moment, counting them out like cards for a game on a table, like birds landing one by one on a wire? I tossed and turned, listening for some terrifying noise on the baby monitor. What if it would all just end today? I'd sit up when I heard a squeak, a sigh, and then the usual deep breathing. Tay-Sachs: the serial killer that takes every moment, one at a time, and unravels it to the beginning, to a scrap of wool that lifts easily in the wind and is shepherded to some unseen place. Lost.

In "The Mentor," another Levin poem, two people turn together to conduct the "science of mourning." This was my great project, mine and Rick's. Two sad scientists putting their heads together the way we once put our son together.

When Ronan's therapist came over on Friday, Good Friday, the first thing she said when she walked through the door was "Crazy wolf moon!" Was it? I had no idea. *I could be living on Mars*, I thought, where there is more than one moon or no moon or moons that move in and out of particular orbits at their moonish, lunar will. I didn't know a thing about Mars. I rarely looked at the night sky anymore. "Pull yourself together," I'd been told and also told myself. What would I pull together? Who was doing the pulling? If I yanked everything together, if I attempted to sweep up the bits and organize them into a whole or a shape or something fit to venture out into the world, I would either disintegrate or explode. Gathering of any kind felt dangerous. I did crave lunar landscapes, like the silvery, shining, pocked earth of Big Bend in West Texas, where from miles away you can see the tiny shadow a scraggly bush makes, knobby fingers stilled in midreach. A ravaged landscape that is unable, by its nature, to keep secrets. I once looked out over the desert in Israel from King Herod's old house at the top of Masada and thought, *No way could David hide here.* In the distance the smallest rock cast a shadow, a little puddle of shade. No secrets, no games, just truth.

The holiday, Easter, which we celebrated only in a secular way (potlucks, chocolate, stuffed bunnies) seemed skeletal. The spring-ready trees were confused, limbs creaking and cold in a tail-end-of-winter breeze on a day when some people would be searching through gardens for Easter eggs and other treasures. *What will next Easter look like?* On a day that was supposed to be about beginnings, my mind had already sprinted to the ending.

How long will he be able to eat? When will the seizures begin? It was lonely being a scientist, even when you had a partner. We took our masks off first. Then our gloves. We took off our clothes and sat in hot cauldrons together, watching our little bowl of grief. We sliced it into strings. We chopped it up. We lit it on fire and ate it. We tied it like ribbons around our wrists and ankles, where it made curious tinkling, chiming sounds. We reasoned that the more dangerous we made things for ourselves, the greater the chance we might get the results we wanted. *Oh, when am I going to own my mind again?* (Jane Kenyon, "Travel: After a Death") Easter, like all holidays, was the enemy that year; it involved calculations. *When. If.* Rick and I returned to our stations, tossed our aprons to the floor (what good are these?), our fingers charred and minds ticking. *There must be something we can do. There must be a solution.* Even a brilliant scientist could not make magic. How many Easter beginnings added up to an ending?

When I was growing up, my parents put together a fantastic Easter egg hunt. My mom must have been padding around in the garden before dawn in her slippers when I could hear my dad taking his shower in the bathroom that shared a wall with my bedroom, getting ready for church. It would be light but still early. We were supposed to have remained quiet and calm and contemplative between Good Friday and Easter morning, but this plan was usually interrupted by the excitement that an episode of *Knight Rider* created in my brother Andy and me on Friday night after the moody service, all dusty purple robes and shaded crosses and my dad's voice speaking the Gospel story offstage, out of sight (and sometimes a bit melodramatically), a disembodied voice waving and swelling over the solemn crowd.

After a fragrant Sunday service with lilies stacked bloom to bloom on the altar in their pink and green and blue foiled pots and everyone in shining clothes and smiles, my brother and I were sent out into the yard at home to search for both the traditional dyed eggs as well as plastic eggs full of clues that would tell part of a story that led to the next plastic egg with the next written clue, another tiny scroll of paper, and finally we'd reach the treasure: a basket full of chocolate and presents, covered in ribbons and bows in pink and blue and yellow. Sometimes the baskets would be inside the dryer, a bathtub, the garage sink. Sometimes the clues made a rhyming poem, a limerick or just a silly little story.

Each day offered a new clue to Ronan's unraveling, which went hand in hand with his growth. He lost his vision as his hair grew longer, a duck tail in the back and enough mop on the top to make a Mohawk with baby oil. He grew teeth that he didn't use except to make him look slightly wolfish when he opened his mouth to eat mushy food. I looked at him carefully, wondering what changes I was missing. If I hovered over his crib and never closed my eyes, would I see his legs and fingers growing longer? What moments would I witness? Would the

growth make a sound? He couldn't move or crawl, but sometimes in the morning he'd be on the other side of the crib. How
long did it take him to move that small amount and at what
cost? What progressions, which in his case were actually re-
gressions, could I track? Would I know when swallowing hurt
him? *How would I know?* I looked and looked and looked like a
mad scientist who hopes never to find what she is searching for.
But looking is not the same as finding, which in turn is not the
same as knowing. It's a question of epistemology, it's a question
of what and how we know.

I once watched a snail move slowly across a road. The
fingertip-sized face was shaped like a bull, two delicate horns
like wet candy. The body was the color of the bright moon
beginning to appear behind me in the summer sky. A little
snail with a little slimy moon head, picking its way across the
road with little pin ears in the dark and in the silence. How did
it know the road would be empty? What did it hear? If it was a
matter of life and death—a car or a hungry dog approaching—
could a snail sprint? How far could it see? What was a horizon
for a snail? If Ronan's brain couldn't flip the image, did that
mean he saw everything upside down?

We know that all of our sensory experiences cry out for in-
terpretation. It's how we *are* in the world and how we understand
who we are, our role, our place. It's what makes us human, what
makes us the animals that we are. This feeling=that reality.

When I was seven months pregnant and in Baltimore to
give a speech at my friend Kaliq's school, we saw a jellyfish ex-

hibit at the aquarium. The precise and patient hitch and pull of these fibrous, filament-like "simple drifters" as they slide to the top of their tanks seemed as mysterious to me as the static hum of the many ultrasounds I'd had up to that point. Each week I was pregnant I watched and listened to Ronan's heartbeat, glowing and insistent and pulsing in what looked like a pool of spilled, vibrating ink. There was something primal about the kicking in my stomach (the baby must move) and the jellyfish moving (they are compelled to move the way they do). What fascinated and repelled me about ultrasounds was the feeling of being turned inside out for examination and the shock I felt each time that heart beat its steady pulse into the quiet exam room, even though I knew it was going going going all the time. I always wondered: *what if it stops?* But I never expected to be alive the moment it did. What I wanted to say as I peered into Ronan's crib was: *Wait. Not yet.* What I also wanted to say was: *Go. Go now before the suffering gets worse.* I kept remembering the jellyfish, and the way they offer the terrifying glimpse into the inner workings of what they are: things made completely visible and the most mysterious of all. Creatures living with their insides on their outsides.

I started to understand that grieving parents are like jellyfish. It's a suspension of belief to get up in the morning, a plodding, creaturely insistence of the clichéd one foot in front of the other methodology of surviving this journey. Each day I felt compelled forward and onward, often against my will. What's unsettling about jellyfish is that we see all the secrets of their bodies and they don't care. We see right through them; we see their scaffolding, the details of their construction, and it does not matter to them, only to us, the lookers, the voyeurs, the witnesses.

I imagined the jellyfish spontaneously swarming to the top of their tank—without consciousness, without attachment or knowledge. I rolled through the grocery store with my floppy, beautiful boy and some days I wouldn't have had it any other way because to wish otherwise would be to wish for another baby, which I did not. On other days I railed against this fact and wished I could pull a jellyfish from a tank and flesh out its mysteries, give it a spine and feet and all the necessary bones, make it walk on land, speak, explain, do the impossible.

Ronan loved the dark blue wrapping paper in his Easter baskets more than the gifts they accompanied. Taking advantage of his best sense, his hearing, the paper was noisy, and bright and bumpy, and although the crackles sometimes made him startle, as all noises did, he kept going for it, turning his head to have a look from the corner of his eye, where his vision was best. I tried, in these moments, as he reached out, to take a mental picture. Eventually he would no longer move; did I have to lose my memory of it, too? In these moments, and when I lingered at the edge of the crib watching him breathe, I felt bottomless with sadness, each breath a fall into a trap door, and I also felt absolutely, euphorically alive.

Spring. A new season, new weather, and yet on one after-noon I walked with Ronan on the path and watched stern pellets of snow, hard and round, melt against his face. I had to sweep one out of the corner of his eye as if it were a remnant of sleep. I watched snow catch on the new blossoms along the path, balance briefly, poise on the tips of cactus needles before rushing on, taken elsewhere by the wind, disappearing.

I opened the blinds of the front window to the sunlight. The street was empty and the house was quiet. My son was being destroyed, every minute of every day, by the lack of one stupid enzyme. What had not yet happened was already happening.

17

It was as if I had stepped free into space

Alone with nothing that I had not
known already.

—Seamus Heaney, "Station Island"

Ronan loved to swim, and it was the activity Rick liked best to do with him. "He looks so calm in the water," he always said. "You can tell he enjoys it." There was so little we could do for our son; this, at least, seemed to please him and make him undeniably comfortable.

In the therapy pool at the community center near our house, Ronan had group swimming time with other kids with developmental disabilities, or "issues," although I often wanted to respond to the therapy pool lifeguard's question "Does your baby have disabilities?" with "Name me a person without a physical issue, and I'll show you a dollar nobody wants." But I always held my tongue and politely said, "Yes, he has several," thinking, *He has every one you can possibly imagine.*

We arrived a bit early for our first therapy session and stood near the locked door of the therapy pool room as kids and their parents began to arrive: a two-year-old girl wearing a hot pink swimming suit, a tiny nine-month-old girl with a fuzz of blond hair (one half of a pair of premature boy-girl twins), a little boy with the thin, unmuscular limbs and stiff movement that I recognized as cerebral palsy, and a boy with a round face and no language—although he didn't need it, because as soon as he got into the pool, his face came alive. He plunged his hands below the surface of the water. His mother kept her arms around him, steadying him as he splashed and kicked. They were both laughing. By the time Rick was ready to walk Ronan down the ramp and into the pool, the humid air and the fact that it was Ronan's nap time had put him to sleep. The life-guard, who looked stunned with boredom, oversaw our "special needs" group. Again, the silliness of these categories. We go on and on in this culture, especially in our schools, about how special every individual child is, how much they matter, and so doesn't it follow that if every kid is so special and unique, then *all* of us have special needs? I splashed a bare foot in the water and thought about, of all things, my trip to Israel six summers before.

I'd gone to Israel to be with a boyfriend I loved and we walked and walked around Tel Aviv and Jerusalem. We visited Masada and King Herod's old crib. We rented a car and drove

to Nazareth, to the Sea of Galilee, a great, clear blue eye surrounded by square apartment buildings. We visited the river
Jordan, site of so many watery submersions and the origin of
much mythology about rebirth and salvation. When I saw the
disappointing strip of brown river, I realized that I'd been
expecting, against all knowledge to the contrary, a clean and
chlorinated pool, like something from an all-inclusive beach
resort. The site of Jesus' tomb was mobbed by a line of tourists
waiting in swaying, impatient lines that reminded me of the
roller-coaster line at Six Flags. I had a craving for a funnel cake,
for fried dough covered in brown sugar, grease soaking through
a paper plate. Outside the church gates, tour guides wearing
black jeans and white shirts waited for their groups, smoking hand-rolled cigarettes in the sunlight. After we entered the
Garden of Gethsemane church through a grove of olives that
looked much smaller than in my imagination, a priest shushed
us violently, his reprimand washing into the high rafters. Walking through the notorious Orthodox neighborhood of Mea
Sharim, sweltering in my long-sleeved shirt, a small boy with
bright blue eyes hissed at me and covered his brother's eyes. The
two boys were under five and dressed in dark suits. They
walked alone—no parents in sight—down cramped streets
running with wind and trash. Printed bulletins begging women
to respect the residents' way of life and dress modestly had
uncurled in the humidity and flew down the streets like errant
paper birds. An empty doll's carriage—a child's lost toy—
hugged against a wall, cornered by wind, before a shift in the

wet breeze sent it careening down the road, its wheels spinning inches above the ground as if in a cartoon. At the Church of the Holy Sepulcher, the assumed site of Jesus' actual crucifixion and entombment, we waited in a long line to see the stone where his body, after it was taken down from the cross, was washed and prepared for burial. By that time I was not expecting to be moved by any of it, and I was not.

Ring around the rosies, pocket full of posies, ashes, ashes, we all fall down. The water therapists belting out this old song from the Great Plague about people dropping dead brought me back into the room, to the pool where kids splashed and cooed and kicked. As Rick descended into the water, the older kids and their parents were already singing in a circle near us.

"You like the water?" I asked Ronan. His face betrayed surprise and then pleasure, the same expressions he made when trying a food for the first time. Rick held Ronan the way our physical therapist taught us: one palm under the head, the other palm under the back, allowing him to glide along the surface. Back and forth, back and forth, his pale and perfect baby body chubby and buoyant, his permanently pointed toes making ribbonlike waves in the surface of the water. His hair spread out around him like pale seaweed. He smiled and kicked when he could. I sat near the edge and dragged my toes back and forth through the water.

Rick explained to the therapist that Ronan's motor skills were locked at a six-month level and that these, too, were already fading. She nodded and touched Ronan's cheek. I was always wary of new people—worried about their reaction to Ronan, ready to strike if they were rude or seemed upset by the way he looked, but she was kind, and she gently took him from Rick and swam with him around the square pool, talking and smiling as Rick and I watched. She looked like a mermaid, swimming with a treasure in her arms, holding it out, preparing to present it to appease some underwater monarch, some beast of the sea.

The kids and their minders (Rick was the only father), bobbed in a circle and sang a welcoming song while one of the therapists passed a ball to each kid, one at a time. *Good morning* (pause) *to Ronan* (pause) *we're glad to see your face, good morning* (pause) *good morning* (pause) *to you.* Jordan, Ashley and Joshua were all greeted in turn. I thought: *I'll bet Ronan is the only one of these kids who is going to die before he turns three.* I felt angry and small and mean. I wanted to leave. I wanted to vomit. I wanted some kind of resurrection that I knew would never arrive.

I watched Rick carefully learning from the therapist how to lift Ronan up and down in the water; how to hold him under the arms and wave his upper body one way so that his bottom half swayed in the other direction, and it went on like that, his torso and then his legs moving from side to side, as if Ronan were swimming or moving on his own, a slow underwater dance.

When Ronan started to whine, letting us know that he was done with swimming for the day, Rick walked him up the ramp and out of the pool. I kept thinking of baptism, of those full-body immersions in the Jordan, or of the *mikveh*, when the whole body goes in one way and comes out different, changed, pure, whole, rearranged, saved, hallelujahed, whatever. At the Dead Sea, which looked about as glamorous as an outdoor pool at an interstate Motel 6, bathers emerged like prehistoric people at the end of the beach where the black mud was deepest, like Adam stepping out of the hand of God, fully formed but completely new. Wet, fresh and covered by mud, his slimy footprint visible on every surface he crossed, Adam was eager to find a mate and name some animals. People waited to use a water hose in the center of the beach to wash off the mud. Wielding it with glee and playfulness, sometimes a bit vengefully, parents and partners and siblings released body after body from anonymity, the second skin rinsing away to reveal freckled shoulders, wacky tan lines and wide hips, misshapen belly buttons, lumpy C-section scars, a middle-age paunch. All the details of the recognizable self.

"He's taking the waters," Rick joked as we drove home, as if Ronan had attended some nineteenth-century bathhouse in order to cure his various upper-class ailments. "If only it were a cure," Rick said quietly, and I avoided looking at his face in the rearview mirror.

When we got home, I put Ronan down for his nap and rode our exercise machine on the highest possible speed to an episode of *Spooks*, the British spy show. Terrorists and bomb threats and back-stabbing politicians, and at the end everything was resolved. Everything was put right.

Watching Ronan float near those other babies, and yet out-side of them, feeling only his body in the water, suspended, his dad's hands supporting him, the echo of laughter and voices, I had one of those moments where the situation I was witnessing had to be a dream or, more precisely, a nightmare.

I had another dream at Yaddo that specifically haunted me in the days and weeks and months after Ronan's diagnosis. One afternoon I fell asleep in the heater-burned air of my small bedroom, listening to the winter rain crackle against the ice-covered trees outside the window. In the dream I sit up and ask, "Where's the baby?" but I am alone. I leave the bed and walk into the kitchen. I have forgotten to put on my leg (and yes, in other dreams I have remembered to do this, remarkably), but the dream mind, ever wise, swiftly crafts a solution: I will float. I am floating in the kitchen and I realize the dining room chairs are hanging from the ceiling or, more specifically, they are hammered to the ceiling, nailed. A ceiling of crucified chairs. The house is empty. The world has been reorganized in some new and terrible way. In the dream I vomit (while float-ing) and the chairs, still nailed up, rock back and forth as I holler into the empty space in a bitchy yet anguished and very Job-like voice, "What's next?"

On my last morning at Yaddo I woke up with that dream print on me—dread in its purest form, a moment of stillness like that single calm beat before catastrophe strikes. I thought of the lines from one of my favorite poems by Sylvia Plath (who, decades before, was also pregnant at Yaddo):

I am calm. I am calm. It is the calm before something awful:
  The yellow minute before the wind walks, when the leaves
    Turn up their hands, their pallors. It is so quiet here.
  The sheets, the faces, are white and stopped, like clocks.
        Voices stand back and flatten.
            —Sylvia Plath,
        "Three Women: A Poem for Three Voices"

The feeling of dread, the flattened voice inside, waiting to howl, waiting to erupt, held on to me. For days I was swaying in dread, gripped by it. I felt as if I'd landed in the wrong place, the wrong *life*. I felt poised for something terrible to happen, for the "what's next?" to reveal itself. Like pain, dread lacks both metaphor and explanation, but I recognized that same feeling as it descended on me in the moments after we received Ronan's diagnosis. *This is happening, this is happening.* The chairs, the floating, the sickness, the dread. Dread is the worst kind of fear, marked, as it is, by an absence of hope. Each day I worked to push it down and intellectualize it as if this might banish it, but like grief, dread's close cousin, its morphology was constantly shifting.

I thought about the dream constantly after Ronan's diagnosis, so annoyed that my big bad expensive brain could not accurately picture or imagine what Ronan's experience might be like, the quality and texture of it. As one neurologist wistfully noted, "We still know very little about the brain."

Ronan had what we called "stations" in the house: his

swing, a lap, the bouncer, the beanbag, the floor for tummy time, which he did for a while, and in one of his backward stages he would lie on his back and lift a hand to touch the stuffed animals swinging from the trapeze above his head, a toy meant for three to six months. All his toys were used in reverse.

Eventually Rick had the sad task of "triaging" Ronan's toys; we decided to put the ones he could no longer use in storage, out of sight. Sitting on the porch I could hear the crunch of plastic, the occasional twitter of a singsong rhyme ("Yankee Doodle," "The Itsy Bitsy Spider," "Twinkle, Twinkle, Little Star) from one of the singing trucks or monkeys or blocks. Just another task we never expected we'd have to do.

The bouncer didn't last long, and soon Ronan could not see the stuffed monkey and the lion swinging from the trapeze, so there was a lot of lap time and "stretchies" on my bent legs, with Ronan lying back like he was in a lounge chair on vacation and working on a tan. The stations of the couch: under an arm, on a lap, snuggled into the corner or enveloped by the beanbag. He might spend twenty minutes moving a soft ball back and forth one inch in one direction and then in the other. There would be other stations, too, and of course, the final one.

In that first year of Ronan's diagnosis I often thought of this station, one of the most beautiful and terrible: Rick walking out of the pool with Ronan in his arms. Water dripped from Ronan's fingers and toes, from the ends of his hair. His father's footsteps created ripples in the water that echoed all the way to the other side of the pool.

18

On Mother's Day, four months after Ronan's Tay-Sachs diagnosis, I tossed out all the old parenting books, all the old certainties and myths. "I felt like I was robbed of time but I didn't have long enough," another dragon mom told me. And although I often said that diagnosis day was the worst day of my life, I knew that Ronan's last day would be worse. When Elliott, the baby closest in age to Ronan, died, I exchanged e-mails with her mother, Becky, who had been my mentor, and she sounded as though she were writing from another planet. Who could bear it?

Who was I as a mother? I tried to be valiant and insightful, but most of the time I thought: *What the hell is going on?* Ronan and I were on this singular path of motherhood-sonhood: one of us knew that the other would not survive. I was supposed to be guiding Ronan through this life and then out of it and into whatever came next, but much of the time I was flailing around in the unfathomable, endless dark, tripping along, occasionally stumbling over a moment of peace, a rough section of ground I hadn't expected, full of knobby tree roots and jutting stones. Making mistakes, feeling focused and angry but achingly free. I felt blind in every possible way: physically, emotionally, spiritually. I also felt switched on, electrified and aware, as if I were on fire or could eat fire or spit sparks, burn something down. Out on the arroyo path with Ronan in the front pack, I often closed my eyes and trudged along, thinking, *It's you and me, little dude, and this is all there is.* It was like stepping through a trapdoor; I dropped and dropped and dropped. I felt a wild clarity, an unstoppable grief and, sometimes, a flash of sadness like a dim memory, as if I had climbed a ladder into a realm of ecstasy I had never experienced before.

In an effort to celebrate mothers (and fathers and administrative assistants and grandparents and Cupid, among others), Hallmark may have a lot to answer for, I'm afraid. Who doesn't feel like crap on these greeting card corporation–sanctioned holidays? Valentine's Day hurts people who receive no Valentines, and gone are the days when you decorated a box in grade school and class rules dictated that everybody at least got something from somebody else. Mother's Day and Father's Day for those who have lost their parents or don't know their parents or feel alienated from their parents feel like long, arduous days where every vision of a family with a mother or father is a stab in the heart. And for those of us who are childless parents

or soon to be childless or have experienced any form of repro-
ductive loss? We keep our little dramas to ourselves, at least in
public, fearing that we'll spoil the party for everyone else and
perhaps add to what already feels like a whopping dose of bad
karma.

I woke up on Mother's Day in the old lodge at Ojo Caliente,
a hot springs mineral spa between Taos and Santa Fe with this
marketing tagline: Soak Your Bones. There were facials and
massages available, but it was the dips in various mineral pools
that promised to cure particular ailments, or at the very least to
make you feel better for the next few hours. (There was, however, no pool for the brokenhearted.) Our room in the lodge
looked exactly like I'd always imagined the postwar hotel room
in J. D. Salinger's story "A Perfect Day for Bananafish." At the
end of the story, the main character shoots himself on the edge
of the bed in light that I imagined would look just like the light
moving into our room on Mother's Day: vaguely beachy, a clear
yellow strong enough to brighten the rustic old furniture and
the dusty carpet floors but not enough to warm them. I thought
about my grandfather, who shot himself in a hot barn when he
was only thirty-five years old. Not exactly an auspicious beginning to my mom holiday. Kids sprinted across the gravel parking lot, yelling and giggling. Birds swooped and hollered,
dipping low and then angling away.

After breakfast Rick and I quietly sat in a mineral bath,
both of us glum. I got an overpriced "relaxing" facial that wasn't
as relaxing as the price suggested. At the beginning of a yoga

class in a warm yurt, when the teacher, standing in a circle of sunlight, asked if there were mothers in the room, I turned and looked out the small window, pretending that I hadn't heard her. Why? Because I knew it might be my last Mother's Day, at least with a child in the picture, and I did not want to explain that to a roomful of strangers taking an all-levels yoga class at a resort facility in the middle of the desert. I scribbled a wish on a piece of paper and hung it on the "wish tree" but didn't believe it would do much good. After all, it wasn't a miracle tree, and if it had been, I wouldn't have believed in it anyway.

Later we watched people of all ages pad across the newly renovated pool area in velvety robes the color of sand. I spotted another amputee in the steam room and remarked to Rick that the man's age and the stunning foot work of his prosthesis suggested that he was an Iraqi war vet. I envied his water leg, which enabled him to jump in the water, two legs and all, without having to find a trusted courier to take the leg back to a deck chair and cover it with a towel so nobody would steal it or spill a drink on it. His girlfriend, tan and toned, posed on the edge of the pool as he snapped photos of her, exclaiming "Gorgeous! I love it!"

Instead of these cheery, flower-laden holidays, what about a day when everyone just cries and mourns and laughs and wails? Memorial Day doesn't cut it. A memorial sounds too strictly ritualistic, too organized. Could we all just please have a big fat day of mourning? Mourning Day. The cards could be blank or sentimental. They could use flowers and lions or dark humor.

They might sing or have pop-up features. The tradition: to sit around and cry over pictures of our loved ones and laugh and tell stories to anyone who would listen and drink strong coffee and fancy tea and elaborate cocktails and cheap wine. Everywhere you went on Mourning Day strangers would tell you about the people they'd lost. You would hear their stories and share your own. You would exchange cards or hugs or cheap little Mourning Day placards with cartoons on them. You wouldn't have to hug or be touchy-feely; you could just talk and laugh and remember, and you wouldn't have to make plans to talk to or see one another again—just that one exchange, those few moments.

Around Memorial Day the news also lit up with stories of soldiers' "alive days." An alive day is the anniversary of a close brush with death, and an opportunity for the living person to celebrate the fact that the date in question is not the one carved into a tombstone or noted on a Wikipedia bio or in an official military letter to loved ones. Soldiers have been celebrating alive days since the Vietnam War, and perhaps for decades before that. They represent a chance to celebrate that an individual has not yet been snatched from this world as we know it, has not yet staggered into the world of "what's next?" whatever that world may be. *Not today,* I told myself. *Not yet.*

On Mother's Day I was a mother, but a different kind of mother, and alien to the qualities, I suppose, that the holiday was created to celebrate. An outsider. My son was a baby and he already had what I thought of as "alive days," his little life always hanging by the weakest, thinnest thread. This strange juxtaposition of holidays and feelings reminded me of the mommy groups/get-togethers/clubs I once attended, where the vibe always felt to me so similar—overly peppy and slightly competitive—as to be dishonest. I never felt entirely comfortable in such groups, maybe because, in most but not all cases, the children seemed to be treated as projects, and even when the mothers were talking about so-called parenting "fails," a smugness crept in.

When I went to my first breast-feeding support group, Ronan was a six-pound, dark-eyed dude dressed in a tie-dyed onesie, screaming his head off unless he was eating (constantly) or sleeping (rarely). I was at a total loss about what to do with him. The other babies were laughing, looking at one another, gumming toys and books and attempting to crawl or just cuddling with their mamas and looking blissful and angelic and sweet. My mother was pawing through the overpriced nursing bras in the "Momma Boutique" in the next room and reminding me that someday I'd be like those moms, and Ronan would be like those other babies: interactive, calm, more of a person than a little red worm. My father was at the Whole Foods down the street buying me a huge pastrami sandwich because I was so emaciated from breast-feeding that I had to eat every twenty minutes. A very nice woman tried to help me use the sling I'd been given as a carrier until Ronan, squirming and shrieking, forced her to say, "He just looks too miserable for this today."

What amazed me in this mom's group was the way the other moms seemed to have it all figured out; they talked confidently about which day care staff was truly aware of the latest trends in child development, which nanny would look after the kids *and* clean the house for a low price ("Look on Craigslist for listings written in broken English! They're the cheapest!"), which coffee shop had the best decaf, which vacation hot spots were the most kid-friendly. I asked them if they were reading any good books, and did they feel, nine months in, as if they had their brains back? No, I was told, but it was good that I was here because if I kept it up, it would mean that Ronan would never have a single ounce of formula. As if that would have been the worst thing in the world, but at the time the prospect of feeding Ronan a sip of formula felt catastrophic. Meanwhile, when I took Ronan to see the gastrointestinal doctor he saw for his reflux, she told me that because of the massive social pressure to breast-feed, "women lie about their breast-feeding habits. Everyone struggles, and very few people can do it exclusively." Had that pack of cheery, organized moms with their snacks at the ready and their boppy pillows and fancy breast-feeding shirts lied to me? Maybe. I never went back.

As a mother of Ronan I had my dragon mamas, a group I was proud to be a part of. These moms knew how to keep it real, and none of them pretended that they knew it all, which was a relief. Politics, religion, class, career aspirations—all of it was meaningless in the face of the experience we shared, the experience of parenting dying kids. These moms were raw and brave and honest enough to ask for help and they cried and raged in public.

On Memorial Day I thought about the kids and babies with Tay-Sachs who had died, those who would die in the next year, and especially the new babies who would be diagnosed and what those parents would experience, that terrible premourning for an inevitable death. The burden of knowing what will happen (although not necessarily in what order) and knowing you will be there to witness it: a kind of death experience, no doubt. Every day was an alive day with Ronan, and built into that celebration was the dark shade of a future Mourning Day. The constant push-pull: here but not for long. What will come next? Why is this happening to my child? Why is this happening to me? Could I still be a mother if I didn't feel uncomplicated joy on the day designed to celebrate the art of mothering?

The year before on Mother's Day, before I knew Ronan was sick, I had attended the requisite brunch of mimosas and pancakes. The next year my mom gave me a locket engraved with Ronan's name and birthdate. Inside is a picture of him, and because I'd been ensconced in Victorian London while reading every Mary Shelley biography I could find, I did as loved ones once did to remember their beloveds: I snipped a piece of Ronan's hair and tucked it inside the locket next to his picture, and promised to wear it forever.

Skip forward a year and in the wake of Ronan's terminal

diagnosis, I was driving to Wyoming with my son in the back-seat when we encountered some truly bizarre weather. A sheet of dust moved both vertically and horizontally across the road, like a wave of heat but grainier, more textured and complicated. I struggled to keep the car steady in the wind. Tumbleweeds were speedweeds, thorny rockets scraping across the wind-shield. Gray clouds hung low and thick in the sky like a plat-form; above and below stretched an expanse of sweet blue sky polka-dotted with cartoonish round clouds. The windmills in the yards of farmhouses we passed looked frantic, spinning so fast they looked like they might fly into the air. The sky was red gold and slightly apocalyptic. But Ronan and I were alive in it, together, headed down the road and straight through the dust and into the oncoming rainstorm. (*I was something orderless in a jar, unable to escape what was happening, unable to get out of what was occurring. All I held on to was that I was not alone.*—Michael Ondaatje, *The Cat's Table*.) A mother and her son. I felt my heart swell into the open road, into the world. If I were to scream, who would hear me? If I rattled the latch of this room, of sadness and panic and inevitability, who would come? Nobody could save us. But on that day we rode through the storm to find streaming from the sky cylinders of sunlight as thick and strong as any downpour and the clear outlines of the mountains in the distance, some of the peaks capped with snow. *Someday I'll be alone on this road,* I thought, *but not yet.* "We're alive," I said out loud. Ronan sneezed in response and let out a cheerful song sigh.

At the end of the day, after we arrived at my parents' house,

Ronan touched the sweet petals of the lilac bush and the branches of the prickly evergreen tree in the backyard. The sky was clear, the air soft. That was Ronan's day of living in this world. One more alive day, and also another day—for both mother and son—closer to death. We could wish it weren't true, we could wish desperately, but we could not have one without the other.

19

And there we were, in a kind of harmony;
and the evening was so beautiful, that it
made a pain in my heart, as when you
cannot tell whether you are happy or sad;
and I thought that if I could have a wish, it
would be that nothing would ever change,
and we could stay that way forever.

—Margaret Atwood, *Alias Grace*

At the crossroads between spring and summer, my friend Carrie brought a burst of hope and calm into our house for two days, a much-needed shot of harmony. We went for a hike in the strangely cold and overcast weather, and I found myself feeling hopeful and frightened at the end of it, with Ronan sacked out in the front pack and his hands pressed to my stomach. Sometimes the soft bulk of him, his solid weight and cellulite thighs, made me jump ahead to the time when my arms would be empty. And then I felt guilty, and then I felt guilty for wasting time feeling guilty when I need to be enjoying my son or else I'd feel guilty about it later.

Carrie's presence was the antidote to this constant circling: being with someone who knows and loves you, someone who can see you from the outside in (and still like you!), is maybe the greatest gift any grieving parent—or person—can expect. Carrie and I used to take long walks in Provincetown, where we met at the Fine Arts Work Center, a working colony for visual artists (Carrie) and writers (me). On those long walks along Herring Cove or Race Point Beach, we talked and talked and lost track of time; when we got back to town, the sun would be setting, the stores closing, and we'd be famished and freezing and desperate for hot chocolate and a hot meal. Six years later, I wished we could hike up a million mountains together, always moving, never tired.

Cultivating an ability to rest in what was an impossible, thorny place—Ronan was dying and he was irreplaceable— was proving very difficult for me as his condition progressed. Without a goal or a solution or something to strive for, something to fight for, I felt lost. There was only today and then tomorrow and then the next day. But waiting was not playing to my skill set, which was about pushing, achieving, driving ahead, meeting this or that goal.

In the words of Grace, a convicted killer with a tortured past and the heroine of Margaret Atwood's stunning and smart novel *Alias Grace:* "It's the middle of the night, but time keeps going on, and it also goes round and around, like the sun and the moon on the tall clock in the parlour. Soon it will be day-break. Soon the day will break. I can't stop it from breaking in the same way it always does, and then from lying there broken; always the same day, which comes around again like clockwork. It begins with the day before the day before, and then the day before, and then it's the day itself . . . The breaking day." Time, time, time: our enemy, and the only friend we have. We need it, long for it, fear it, loathe it, dream about it, try to extend it and shrink it.

Coming to peace with "nonaction," I realized, felt impossible. I was used to doing and moving. Now I was waiting and thinking. Writing. Crawling up over the edge of each breaking day, broken but ready for action. Aching with fear and also brimming with a bright, swollen fearlessness. Fueled by a new ambition: to be still, to consider, to examine. It was against my nature, but my nature was changing. I was living an oddly litur-gical life: examining grief with thought, word and, occasion-ally, a hell of a lot of movement.

At the end of May my friends Amy and Jennifer hosted a fund-raiser for Ronan, a spin class followed by yoga (called the Ronan-a-thon) and I was given the opportunity to sweat and stretch and move and cry in honor of my son, and I didn't do it alone. I've gotten a lot of guff about my penchant for exercise, which, yes, is an obsession, yes, is an addiction, and, yes, can be a crutch. But it is also recommended on a daily basis by various celebrity doctors, health councils, and the American Academy of Doctors of This That or the Other Organ.

I took spin and yoga classes with the same group of women fives times a week for four years in Santa Monica. We obsessively claimed our bikes next to one another in the spinning room; there were songs we loved and others we rolled our eyes about; we lent one another socks and offered swigs from water bottles; we were tirelessly coached by the indefatigable Amy to the sounds of Metallica and Journey and Bon Jovi and AC/DC; and then we relaxed and stretched by the poetic instruction of Jen and her magical lavender oils and head massages. We didn't discuss the gritty particulars of our lives, and in that sense we were like stereotypical "guy friends" who like to do things together rather than talk about feelings/relationships/life/other complications. Adult playdates, but without the cocktails or conversation. We groaned about being asked to do yet another set of sit-ups. We chanted om and then flopped onto our yoga mats. Like all self-respecting gym rats, we then crawled to the showers, feeling spent and stinky, before going on with our individual lives. Until that weekend in May I knew very little about the present realities of these women, let alone their old stories, their old wounds.

When Ronan was diagnosed, some of my friends ran from it and I guess some of them are still running. Months later some admitted that they didn't know what to say, how to respond, and I understood this reaction as deeply as I had trouble forgiving it. My friends from the gym, however, women I hardly knew in the sense that we didn't share many personal stories, came right at me: with e-mails, an envelope full of checks for future medical bills, concerned voice and text messages. I was surprised at first, but then I realized that I viewed these connections as if they were superficial, as many of my "why are you going to the gym when you could be thinking (that is, doing something important)?" friends casually assumed.

But consider this: I saw these women almost every day for four years. I did push-ups with them during every day of my pregnancy, up until the day I delivered Ronan. When I told people familiar with grief that in some sense Ronan died for me on the day of his diagnosis, they warned me about the grief to come when my son was physically gone. "You carried him for nine months," my friend Chris, also a writer, reminded me, and as strange as it might seem, so did the women in that gym. No, we weren't having some deep intellectual experience, but we were having an experience. The difference? It was embodied. It was, in a sense, mindless. What a relief.

All of our most ecstatic, profound experiences (in addition to some of the most terrifying and destructive) are lived in the body. I vividly remember the first expert run I skied in Winter Park in the early 1980s. Moguls like giant fists as high as my waist, the bottom of the hill an icy slide straight to the bottom. I was sweating even before I shot off the top of the mountain, my coach screaming at me (but in the nicest and most supportive way) that I was ready to do this and if I believed in myself I would finish without breaking my neck. *Go, Emily, go!* My heartbeat swished frantically in my ears; my heart was a rocket burning an upward path through my chest, and my leg and arms went to jelly and then to steel and then back again over each hump. On and on, until the end of the run, and when I looked up and saw where I had come from, I didn't think, *Look what I can do,* which has a built-in superiority (itself an inferiority complex in disguise) and seems to be the guiding principle of disabled sports (and of all competitive sports, actually), but I observed what my body could feel and experience in that moment. The feeling was freedom—of the most profound kind. You know what else? During that entire twenty minutes I didn't have a single thought, and I've probably never been happier. Exercise as an experience, as the joy of embodiment.

Why are we so afraid of the body? Is it because it's a mess, unpredictable, mortal, unreliable? We take pains to perfect it, to keep it healthy, but we probably wouldn't go to such extremes if we weren't scared to death to lose it. A paradox: we pretend we don't need it, that it's our minds that matter, and yet the body is the thing we can't ignore and that knocks our thinking minds flat to the floor.

During my four-year writer's block in Los Angeles, I thought I needed to leave the body in order to figure out what the hell was going on with my writing life. I needed to chuck the monkey mind, the constant cycling, the endless *thoughts.* So during a three-month sabbatical from teaching, I took a meditation course in Santa Monica. The teacher annoyed me, in part because rather than letting us practice meditation, he seemed intent on talking about the electromagnetic forces at work in the universe (something about comets?) and the new world order, of which we'd all be taking part whether we liked it or not. Frankly, I thought he was full of shit, especially when I was trying to sit quietly for twenty minutes while imagining a lit candle floating in front of my third eye, which I still wasn't certain I'd successfully located. "We are moving from the age of energy into the age of matter," he postulated. "It's these living bodies that will save us." Okay, maybe salvation is a stretch, but several years later I considered that he might have had a point.

Flying into Los Angeles for Ronan's fund-raiser, I saw that massive grid, the straight lines of boxy houses with their swimming pools like blinking blue eyes. When I touched down, I had just read this line from the novel *Year of Wonders*, by Geraldine Brooks, a novel about the Great Plague of 1665, and also about what happens to people—how they twist and bloom—during catastrophe. "These memories of happiness are fleeting things, reflections in a stream, glimpsed all broken for a second and then swept away in the current of grief that is our life now. I can't say that I ever feel what it felt like then, when I was happy. But sometimes something will touch the place where that feeling was, a touch as slight and swift as the brush of a moth's wing in the dark." I felt the joy of familiarity at the sight of palm trees and pesky traffic snarls. I got in my rental car, sped onto the 405 freeway—which was already a parking lot at three o'clock in the afternoon—and cranked up the cheesiest, bubble-gum hip-hop pulsating rhythm I could find. I drove with all the windows rolled down and needlessly used my horn at least three times on the short drive south to Long Beach. The shimmering concrete, the fancy cars, the sun sun sun, the skyline muddled by pollution, the deceptive sea-salt smell of air ranked as some of the unhealthiest in the nation. I didn't care. I inhaled that smell of burning asphalt and over-crowded, overindulged West Coast city. I've been nomadic all my life, rootless, and I always savor these brief glimpses of what it feels like to be grounded. I was on my way to the house of my friends David and Lisa; I was headed to mojitos and tapas in a sun-drenched bar, to conversation and late-night kebabs and expensive brandy. I was approaching one of my homes.

There is power in a gathering, big or small. It's why houses of worship exist. It's why we have parties to celebrate, to mourn, to just be. At the beginning of the Ronan-a-thon, Amy asked us to imagine a collective heartbeat. For more than an hour, a roomful of sweating bodies, pounding blood, and a united em-bodied intelligence focused on my son. (And oh so many Springsteen songs and power ballads. "Don't Stop Believin'!" Never!) We were not riding for a cure because there wasn't one; we were riding for Ronan's life. A celebration, a tribute. Time stopped—painfully, beautifully. A crystalline moment wal-loped right down in the middle of a pile of tumult.

During the yoga class, when my friend Jen asked us to open our hearts out wide for a baby that some of the people practic-ing that night had never met, I thought: *This might be what it's like to be Ronan.* Every moment a wonder, every moment distilled.

Stopped. Each moment out of time, with no memory attached, and with only the body as the guide, the gauge of experience. I learned that you don't need to know much about another person's grief in order to share it and help him or her bear it. People can be amazing and resilient and giving when they don't have to be. Hearts can pound right out of bodies; they can *move*. It's not gross or alien or weird at all; it's human.

More than anything else, I felt accompanied. Me with all my words, so many words, so many I couldn't keep up with them, and here were people, in the sweat and silence and effort, who could just stay there. They could cry for Ronan when I could not. There was a fullness in that emptiness, a literal, visceral feeling of life in death; finally, when so many days felt like the reverse. We went out for cocktails and steaks and we laughed and I learned about these women I had sweated with for four years—things I didn't expect, both the funny and the painful. We could be sad but also celebratory. It was an important lesson for me.

As I left Los Angeles, the waves were like chalk marks drawn on the surface of the water. Flying over New Mexico, the plane hung in the air and the wing shuddered still for a moment despite the notorious winds sheering off the Sangre de Cristo Mountains. A maze of empty roads twisting into land and sky. We descended into the home-for-now and back into the situation of my life, which, for the next few years, would no doubt feel a bit like living on a foreign planet. The planet of grief, where love and loss exist and occur in equal measure. Like

Anna, the heroine of Brooks's novel who loses both her sons to the plague: "I knew that it was true that fear of losing him had marched beside that love, every moment of the short time I had him with me."

Grief isn't just an alternative universe, it's the nastiest, cattiest, meaner-than-a-slighted-and-jealous-mean-girl snake. It's not a cute garden snake that slithers under rocks and looks, in its own snakish way, cuddly. Grief is a cobra. It is fierce, it hides, lurks, strikes, and it can be brutal or even fatal. And it is lived in the body; it can be seen and felt and touched. It is not an intellectual experience but a bodily one. As Bashō says:

> Come, see
> Real flowers
> Of this painful world.

Grief can be seen, felt, touched and tasted. Plucked. Chewed. My mind was trying to keep my heart together, to steel it, but I realized that a broken heart might be more useful because it's fluid, cracked, full of room, messy, without defined contours or corners. It lacks certainty, and therefore judgment. Jen gave me a clear white rock that is solid but also transparent in places. Maybe the ability to break is what can heal it. Maybe Yeats got it wrong; the center *can* hold, especially when it doesn't have a choice.

20

Grief is like a long valley, a winding valley
where any bend may reveal a totally new
landscape . . . Sometimes the surprise is the
opposite one you are presented with, exactly
the same sort of country you thought you
had left behind miles ago. That is when you
wonder whether the valley isn't a circular
trench. But it isn't. There are partial
recurrences, but the sequence doesn't repeat.

—C. S. Lewis, *A Grief Observed*

That summer I sat at a great wooden slab of a writing desk
in southern Spain, on a retreat with other writers, looking out over a hump of mountain crowned with lights. Earlier
that day, dropping through the thick layer of clouds, a hoop
skirt of sunshine opened like the bones of a parasol but offered
no shade. It was summer solstice, and that night there would be

a bonfire on the beach and free sardines *(gran sardinada!)*, live music and booze and "treats for kids." Noche de San Juan. *Equinocio*—the equinox. People would throw what they wanted to cast off into the fire, little sins or sadnesses scribbled onto slips of paper and scooped up in the blaze. I had nothing to burn and everything to lose. I was not in the mood for fiestas. Instead I sat reading C. S. Lewis and writing about Ronan.

C. S. Lewis knew how to do grief: how to write it, how to think about it, and how to live through it and finally dwell in it. Originally published under a different name, the sleek little missile of a book is the almost journalistic chronicle of the minutes and seconds and hours and weeks and months of grief after the death of Lewis's beloved wife, a woman he fell in love with late in his life and much to his brooding but delighted surprise. He married her while she was ill, fully aware that their time together was limited. The book is angry, profound, wrenching and, above all, full of questions that Lewis attempts to answer using both faith and intelligence together, a pairing that feels wholly unexpected, a colorful weasel popping out of an ordinary cardboard box. What's a devout Christian guy (indeed, an *apologist*) to do with a big fat heap of despair when the God he believes in has arranged for a fabulous, postresurrection afterlife that doesn't accommodate despair and actually might equate it with sin? He digs and digs with the sharp instrument of his mind. He's a virtual cutter, and he will not let the difficult topics lie. He goes right for them.

Grief is a sickness, Lewis reasons, and a deadly one without a cure—"Meanwhile, where is God? This is one of the most disquieting symptoms"—and he searches his formidable, very wise and devout brain for answers or cures that might include the notion of a good (or bad) God, the time-space continuum and logic. He comes up short in every respect. He is dizzy, whirling, lost and sad, but he does not give up. He thinks and thinks and thinks. Each day he goes back, each day he wrangles: why, where, how, when, what? Do people (their bodies, their minds, their "sum totals," whatever we might mean by that) become "sheer intellects" in our minds and memories, able to peer through our enchantments and reveal our self-delusions? Do dead spirits become ghosts housed in memory or are they actually physical ghosts, and if so, are they chain-rattling and pesky, floating about in the dead of night, or are they calm and contented fairies fluttering about? Are the long-dead beloveds wandering through Kafka's letters actually real? If one begs God for mercy, does that mean that God is capable of withholding it, and what does that say about the quality or effectiveness of God's mercy in the first place? How is God truly merciful if, in every case, he's making a choice? It's like love: you don't decide to be in, you *fall* into it or else it's not love but something else entirely. Lewis lets it all fall into his head and then out again. He is a shackled journalist seeking to write a factual article without the opportunity to gather any evidence or empirical proof or even move off the floor of some smelly old prison in some faraway place. All he can do is scratch on the walls and wonder and writhe around on the bare floor. The only place to search, the only landscape he can visit, is his heart. Turns out that's a pretty big and interesting place.

Why is his method of thought so interesting, so new? In the middle of his grief experience, Lewis acknowledges the limits of empathy. We are constantly told (and sometimes taught, if this is possible) to be empathetic, to develop empathy, to use it when thinking about or talking about another person's difficult situation. It's like a marketable skill, something to deploy, detonate, *use*. We are asked to extend our empathy (or, more accurately, our sympathy, which is more of a distancing maneuver) almost every day. Tsunamis. Terrorist attacks. Bombs. Famines. Hurricanes. Child abuse. Rape. War. We get facts and are asked to imagine and we say *isn't that terrible* and we believe that we empathize. *I feel you*, we say, and *the world is wicked* and *I'm so sorry*. Nice theory, Lewis concludes; too bad the whole notion of empathy is completely bunk. "You can't really share someone else's weakness, or fear or pain." You can't really test the strength of a rope until you're asked to hang from it over a cliff. There have to be stakes. After his wife dies, Lewis understands that nobody—ever—can feel another person's agony. *Not even God.* It is this last bit that makes him truly weary, as prayer (his old standby) has become useless to him. If God has limits, then what?

Without prayer to sustain him, Lewis is stranded *in* (not *by*) grief, and, what's worse, it's a landscape of his own making, and the geography is constantly shifting. It's a place, sure, but nobody can come and visit; nobody has the password, nobody can really, truly walk through that wardrobe door and see what you're doing on the other side of it, or what you've been imagining or experiencing. Grief as a place is textured and variable in terms of weather, chance inhabitants, and geographical location. It might be lunar, alpine, subtropical. It might have birds or beetles or very large and hungry bears roaming about, hunting. It might be a house, an apartment, a mansion, a shack. Each day requires a reorientation, a brutal schooling in the vicissitudes of grief:

> Man dwells when he can orientate himself within and identify himself with an environment, or, in short, when he experiences the environment as meaningful. Dwelling therefore implies something more than "shelter." It implies that the spaces where life occurs are places, in the true sense of the word. A place is a space which has a distinct character. Since ancient times the genius loci, or "spirit of place," has been recognized as the concrete reality man has to face and come to terms with in his daily life.
>
> —Christian Norberg-Schulz, *Genius Loci:*
> *Towards a Phenomenology of Architecture*

You inhabit grief and grief inhabits you, which means you have to learn how to dwell within it. The problem with this is that each time you open a door or look behind a pretty-looking tree there's something terrible and stinking and life-threatening flowering behind it.

As Lewis navigates his feelings of being cursed (his beloved wife gone at forty-five), he realizes that grief is a mobile landscape and it's not wholly bad or to be avoided. Yes, you never know when it might show up at your door and start planting some rotting trees or tasteless garden gnomes. You also don't know when you'll notice a perfect, blooming rose, or experience a moment of utterly uncomplicated happiness that no drug could provide. But I still felt deeply afraid. I felt the yawn of some terrible loss that was to come, that had, in some respects, already arrived, a gravitational tug of pure, unadulterated horror. Lewis: "No one ever told me that grief felt so like fear. I am not afraid, but the sensation is like being afraid. The same fluttering in the stomach, the same restlessness, the yawning. I keep on swallowing." Yes, I thought, yes. Being in the world while grieving, while holding the "doomed" child in front of you or thinking about that child, means that you moved through the world tired, or uncaring, indifferent and detached, as if you were slightly drunk. Prayer may seem pointless to Lewis—"But when you go to Him when your need is desperate, when all other help is in vain, what do you find? A door slammed in your face, and a sound of bolting and double bolting on the inside"—but thinking and imagining *do not.* He gets up and gets right back into his landscape of grief. He starts planting, weeding, tearing up, building, burning everything to the ground and starting over.

In *A Grief Observed*, in the middle of all his spiritual and intellectual activity, Lewis gets technical; he searches, flounders. What happens to the physical body, he muses, and/or to the soul, to the *person*, this "cloud of atoms," after death? "That is, *in what place* is she *at the present time?*" Part of what infuriates Lewis about the "she's in heaven" angle is that it presumes that his beloved wife is either static, and therefore might as well be dead, or alive, and then how does that work? Does she age in the way we understand it in our own universe and in our own bodies? Or is there reverse aging? Do we morph into various creatures at various angelic whims? "Jung said that there is no coming to life without pain, and that may well be true of what happens to us after death. The important thing is that we do not know. It is not in the realm of proof. It is in the realm of love." Is there some death initiation? Some physical or moral hoops? How can we ask a God to be both mysterious and all-powerful and also understandable? "All nonsense questions are unanswerable. How many hours are there in a mile? Is yellow square or round?" Lewis is an algebra teacher trying to explain the actual physical size of an imagined number—is it the size of a basket, a kitten, an ocean, the microscopic head of a pin?

Kind people have said to me, "She is with God." In one sense that is most certain. She is, like God, incompre-

hensible and unimaginable . . . Unless, of course, you
believe all that stuff about family reunions "on the further shore," pictured in entirely earthly terms. But that is
all unscriptural, all out of bad hymns and lithographs.
There's not a word of it in the Bible. And it rings false.
We know it couldn't be like that. Reality never repeats.
The exact same thing is never taken away and given back.

No alternative realities, then. No Ronan growing up in
some other dimension, on some other planet or in some other
place, in some imaginary heaven. But then why the dreams of
his walking into my room and asking for a story, a glass of
water, a hug, asking for comfort after a nightmare? Why these
images of him at six, ten, sixty, thirty-two? Why were the images so vivid? Had part of him already crossed over and these
dreams were a glimpse of a parallel universe not unlike the one
Lewis creates behind the wardrobe door? And how could I
square a nonbelief in God's existence with this desire to blame
God for not being good, for allowing evil, and for demanding
that some part of my son go on after his physical death? Lewis:
"What reason have we, except our own desperate wishes, to
believe that God is, by any standard we can conceive, 'good'?
Doesn't all the *prima facie* evidence suggest exactly the opposite.
What have we to set against it?" But then who or what creates
the afterlife, the secondary world, the other place? He revises
this logic in the next chapter, describing it as "a yell" instead of
a thought, and in the end he decides that the depiction of God

as sadist is too anthropomorphic to be an adequate description of God's alleged powers, even more inaccurate and offensive than an old bushy-bearded man looking out for humankind's best interests.

Of course, like Lewis, I would never *not* be without Ronan, from the moment after his last moment and until the final moment of my own life. His absence, like Lewis's wife was for him, would be "like the sky, spread over everything."

C. S. Lewis would have likely identified with this passage from *Frankenstein: Why did I not die? More miserable than man ever was before, why did I not sink into forgetfulness and rest? Death snatches away many blooming children, the only hopes of their doting parents: how many brides and lovers have been one day in the bloom of health and hope, and the next a prey for worms and the decay of the tomb! Of what materials was I made, that I could thus resist so many shocks, which, like the turning of the wheel, continually renewed the torture?*

I realized, with horror and despair and with a strange, breathtaking relief, that life would always be amiss in some way. And also that I would never forget Ronan; that it would be impossible. There were a lot of mountains in the land of grief, a lot of gut-busting treks, a lot of *work* to do: tunnels and high rises to dig and build; tourist attractions to promote. And that needed to be done on a daily basis, mind you, because the beloved died again and again. Rebuilding was always required. It's easy to get lost in the work of creating a whole new country of grief, and Lewis worried about the days after the "mad midnight moments." I, too, dreaded the moment after the final moment, that "landfall," as Lewis would describe it (different from an "arrival," which implies safety). No wonder grieving people are so exhausted all the time; no wonder we retreat to trash television and episodes of *Law and Order* or hypomanic episodes or liters of vodka or brief and lurid love affairs with people we hardly know. Especially in this culture where we're taught that all of our value rests, somehow, in the future and what we do or accomplish there, what do we do when what's coming for us is death?

If it is impossible to truly care about the sorrows of the world until they are our own, as Lewis claims, meaning that our faith and sympathy are revealed for what they truly are— acts of imagination—then what? Imagination is okay, Lewis decides. It is all we have; it is enough. When the grief lifts, he remembers his wife best; when he is not thrashing and screaming, he can feel her, he can rest, he's at peace. The intensity of our longing to understand, he believes, is what makes that understanding so uniquely impossible.

That night in Spain as one season drained into another, I listened to dogs barking all night, goats bleating wearily from hillsides. *There is nothing I understand,* I thought, and finally, after days of thinking and writing and ruminating—the exercise of the grief-stricken—I fell asleep.

21

The world of dew
is the world of dew
and yet, and yet—

—Kobayashi Issa
    (after the death of a child)

In September, Rick and I took Ronan on a routine visit to
the neurologist. Another trip to the Mind Center, to the
drab strip mall sprawl of Albuquerque, the air ten degrees hotter than Santa Fe, the roads at least one lane wider. The sky was
clogged with smoke from the various fires that had been raging
across New Mexico for nearly a month, since mid-June. The
horizon was choked by a haze that swallowed the view of the
Jemez and Sangre de Cristo mountains. Fire was crossing state
lines; smoke was drifting across borders.

In the waiting room at the neurologist's office we sat with
Ronan and Skipit, the "ultra soft" light blue dog toy with elon-

gated arms and legs that made him look like a stretched-out bunny. We watched kids with normally developing brains scribble with crayons at a small table in the corner. Rick cradled Ronan's head in his hands and let his body rest on his forearms. I rubbed Skipit the dog-bunny over Ronan's hands and he blinked his pale-lashed eyes. Five and a half teeth were visible when he smiled.

The nurse walked us into the vitals room and weighed Ronan in a bucket (twenty-four pounds), probed gently with an ear thermometer to take his temperature, measured his head (in the seventy-fifth percentile) and briefly left the room to get a cuff small enough to fit around Ronan's arm to measure the pressure of his blood moving through the hidden highways of baby veins hidden by fat.

"You have a monkey, a giraffe and a lion on your shirt!" I told him. "And your shirt is green!"

"Uhn-gee!" he replied, and squirmed a bit on Rick's lap.

Back to the main waiting room, into another smaller waiting room, then into the actual examination room, and finally the doctor appeared with two interns in tow, telling us that this was a "teaching hospital" and that these soon-to-be doctors were here to learn. Tay-Sachs kids in New Mexico—and really, in most places—are like unicorns. Nobody has seen one although they are rumored to exist. *I don't want anyone sizing up my child as if he's little more than a science project,* I thought when I saw the eager, scrubbed faces of these interns. The smell of aftershave floated into the room.

I was wary of those newbies, those docs-in-training, having been prodded and treated like a strange specimen of a body by interns before, like a body under a microscope in the lab, but when I looked at Rick, he seemed willing. I reminded myself that this was not just about me, or even just about Ronan. What if these doctors were able to help a Tay-Sachs kid some-day because of what they learned here? I was not a child any-more; if they got rude or inappropriate I would ask them to leave. But they were kind, and at least one of them was ener-getic and genuinely interested. He sidestepped all the annoying platitudes of "I can't imagine" and "I don't know how you do it." He asked us how we were doing and didn't flinch at the answers. The other intern sat in a chair near the door taking notes, as silent as a fearful ghost, although he looked spooked. Maybe he had a hangover, I postulated. Or maybe he'd been up for thirty-six hours straight. They asked questions, we an-swered, they nodded. Rick talked a lot at doctor's appoint-ments; he was nervous, I think, and sad. He gave the full picture of what was happening with Ronan, down to the smallest de-tail. His attention to our child was almost sacramental. The devil is in the details—and in sadness as well.

The doctor checked Ronan's reflexes. We explained that he wore splints at night to keep his feet flexed and eliminate spasms in his knees—little flashes of electricity just beneath his dimpled skin—that happen when the feet are constantly pointed. The splints were decorated with a school of brightly colored fish swimming in a deep blue plaster background above and below the white Velcro straps. When these were fitted at the prosthetist's office, Ronan's feet were marked with blue pencil. I remembered being marked with lipstick around my hips, my crotch, my ass, lines like thin red smiles, like skinny, bloody wounds drawn on my body as guides for where the leg should hit, where things should bend and match up, where parts of the made part of the body were supposed to go. All the seams made visible. I was the creature and the prosthetist was Dr. Frankenstein slaving over his creation, fitting all the pieces of my body together, trying to make it right. The prosthetist and his assistant worked in silence, and when they left the room, I flipped over the lipstick tube to look at the name of the color— "Cherries in the Snow." I used to watch those lipstick scars float off in the bath, as if the water were a handkerchief that could just lift them away. *Kiss kiss, blot blot* and the red bloomed like blood from a wound in the water. Washed away, washed out. It took a few days for the blue marks to wash off Ronan's feet and ankles. The splints didn't seem to bother him.

The intern nearest the door flipped the light off and fumbled with his eye light, and for a moment the five of us plus Ronan were sitting in darkness. "Gee," Ronan said softly and kind of creepily in his scratchy voice.

"Ooh, haunted hospital room," I chirped, but my voice was too brash, too loud. "Ghost baby," I said, and then felt sick that I'd said this.

The doctor peered into Ronan's cherry-red eyes in the darkness—I watched his eyelashes blink, skinny shadows, two feathery doors opening and closing on his cheeks, the curved and shining whites of his eyes, their kaleidoscope colors obliterated by the bright light.

The lights went back on and we all looked at Ronan. "He seems so well loved, like just another member of the family." We nodded and stared at each other. I thought about Frankenstein's wretch watching a family from his perch outside the house, in the cold, and I felt myself grow hot and defensive, about to ask, "Well, of course he's part of our family; what else would he be? What are we supposed to do? Just abandon him? Kick him under the bus?" But I understood that the doctor's intentions were kind, and that he probably felt as helpless as we did. He was a brain specialist and there was nothing he could do but tell us why seizures happen and then write a prescription. He probably felt useless, helpless and stupid. We knew how he felt. There was no future to discuss. Ronan wasn't going anywhere but back home with us—home, where the rooms of Sol y Luz Street belonged to him. No doctor would barge through the door of the exam room with a miracle cure. No amount of words could fill the great space between our parenting experience and the doctor's. He wrote us a prescription for a suction machine, I asked if that would be categorized under durable medical equipment in insurance billing lingo, he said he thought so, and then I reiterated—in a bratty tone I had meant to be much nicer—our decision not to use a feeding tube. More silence. We decided to come back in November. In the smaller waiting room in front of the bigger waiting room where the same kids were still working on the same crayon photos (I watched them through the window in the door), the sweaty-faced receptionist pulled up her giant, complicated computer scheduler on an enormous screen and said, "Okay, Mom, which day do you want?" This question filled me with a dark dread; I thought of the kids who had died of Tay-Sachs already this year. I thought about Ronan's place in "the waiting room," and that one day would be his day. Flowers and food and condolences would arrive at the house. Ronan would be buried or cremated. There would be a memorial. He would be gone.

On the way home my eyes started to burn from the smoke. My throat felt dry, chapped. The sky was a hazy, pale blue, the color of Skipit, who was tucked under Ronan's arm. "The fires are killing my eyes," I said to Rick, who sat reading a book next to a snoozing Ronan.

"Do you need to pull over?" he asked. I did not. We didn't want to do this. Nobody wanted to do this. Ronan wouldn't always be in the waiting room; it was going to be his turn to go through that door soon enough, too soon. *Which day do you want?* What a terrifying question.

In the afternoon Ronan sat next to me while I read in the comfort of the swamp cooler. Outside, the sky was low and muddled. Ronan sat on my lap like the toddler he'd be if he could toddle. His head notched between my chin and collarbone, his arms stretched up around my neck, and I held him as if he'd just come running to me with a skinned knee or a hurt feeling. I said, "It's really okay," as if he'd asked me if it was going to be. His skin was soft and his hands were sticky. His mouth smelled sweet. The back of his head was sweaty, ringlets twisting around his earlobes. I held him and inhaled his sweaty-baby-Ronan scent and remembered Rick telling the neurologist, "We're not totally convinced he knows who we are," and I thought about what an injustice it was. I'd heard so many fathers say to me over the years, "Oh, I don't really like parenting," or they didn't say anything at all or they were just absent phantom dads, ghost fathers, shitty selfish fathers. Rick's fathering, this great gift, felt wasted, even though I knew this was an incorrect assessment. How could love be wasted? And how could Ronan not deserve it? What was unconditional love if not love that expects nothing in return, especially from a child who was arguably as helpless as Ronan? We made him, we loved him, end of story. He expected our unconditional love, he got it, and he was not locked in guilt or conflicted about it. I reminded myself that unconditional love asks nothing back; being Ronan's mom was my giant, painful opportunity to learn this. What I was being asked to do felt both entirely instinctive and completely impossible. To live the reverse of Shelley's Dr. Frankenstein, to love my child without limits or expectations. Years from now he would not be chasing me down, asking "Why didn't you love me?" He will be dead, and I will have been his mother. It wasn't the story of motherhood I expected to tell, but sitting there on that hot afternoon I felt I could claim it. I had to. Firefighters who spring into the blaze to save people are not brave; they have no choice.

Firefighters in New Mexico had set controlled burns around particular fires—they started smaller fires in order to control the biggest ones, to prevent them from raging out of control. These controlled backburns were essential for containment. Real or set, in both cases the trees ended up charred husks, row upon row of smoking skeletons made of bark and ash.

Ronan and I rolled to the coffee shop to read the paper, check the status of the Los Conchas fire near Los Alamos, the multicolored maps printed on the front page of the local papers. I learned that fifty years ago Ernest Hemingway had shot himself in the head. His behavior up until that point had become increasingly erratic and paranoid. In Casper, Wyoming, he tried to walk into a propeller when the plane he was traveling in landed for refueling. In Spain I'd felt the tip of the propeller against my cheek, the cool, bright point of that blade.

In that same newspaper I found these stories: the parents of an abused girl were given prison sentences that could never be long enough. The girl was fourteen and had maggot-infested bedsores and weighed forty-five pounds. She had cerebral palsy and was mentally retarded. The murderers of a seven-year-old girl who was dumped in a ditch in 1958 were found. Her family lamented the loss of this "athletic and beautiful" girl who was "going to be something." I read another story about migrants who were brutalized on the journey to the United States from Mexico and Central America. One of them asked the reporter, "Should I go back? What do you think?" On another page I learned that a lock of President Lincoln's hair was expected to be worth about $35,000 at an upcoming auction.

There are so many rooms in the house of grief, so many basements without lights or windows, and so many people inside waiting to go somewhere else, to cross some border, to live, to die. You choose a particular door and you cannot go back, you cannot walk back through it. I closed the paper and closed my eyes and put my hand on Ronan's arm. *Still here, he's still here.*

That little girl who died of starvation and maggot-infested sores was a human being. So was the little girl with "potential" who was murdered and dumped in a ditch. So were all the nameless, faceless people traveling on hot trains and being raped and robbed and beaten trying to get to this country, which would brutalize them further. They were human beings. To be valuable they didn't need to have so-called potential, whatever that means. Earning power? Advanced degrees? Exciting inventions in their pockets? Beautiful bodies that might sell products and have the added value of boosting the economy? And they lived, even though their lives were truly the stuff of other people's nightmares. Their stories mattered, even if we never heard them. Ronan's life mattered, even though I was the one telling his myth, even though his brain was devastated, his body doomed. Sitting at Java Joe's with Ronan on my lap, I read those stories and felt myself flinch. Yes, I am a writer, but it is not the sum of who I am. We are not what we become, how we look, what we do—are we? Because Frankenstein's monster was driven to murder, was he only a murderer and nothing more, only a monster? Or was he just a grieving son? And his father grieved, too—that he'd failed him, failed to see the beauty in the creation of his own hands, this wretch he assumed he could never love or understand and therefore never tried to know before it was too late.

Who counts in this world and how much? Who does the deciding? Who has "potential" (that is, value) and who does not? On the patio, thunder rumbled in the distance and Ronan squirmed against my chest, complaining a bit. What did matter was love, given freely and without agenda or expectation. I loved Ronan, this unique person, this human being, without thought to what it might lead to for me, what it might say about me, or what it made others think about me. It didn't matter if people thought the situation was tragic or the saddest thing in the world, or they thought I'd gone wild with grief or become a mean and manic bitch. So what? This was *my* son, my baby, my "handful of earth," sitting on my lap, cooing and squawking into an approaching thunderstorm under a dropped and thickening sky, the wind whipping through his hair as if he were on a roller coaster, feeling the fresh change in the air. Oh, I loved him. But that love would not chain him. There was nothing expected of or for him. In that love he was free. A love that was settled and calm, with no more thinking to do. A love that left people speechless, confused, delirious with misunderstanding.

Last year on July Fourth, Ronan snored through the fireworks that boomed through our Los Angeles neighborhood, rattling the thin walls of our studio apartment. We went to a pool party in the Palisades and I bounced him as he screamed and then, in a rare moment of calm, chatted over his head to a friend. A different year, another life. In these nine months a new world had bloomed, terrible and true.

Fireworks were discouraged in Santa Fe due to fire season and the drought, but there was still a sanctioned city display visible from our backyard. Rick and I watched a few explode in the middle distance, and then we went inside, slowly closing the door that leads into the house, careful not to wake our child sleeping in his room.

22

By scribbling I run ahead of myself in order
to catch myself up at the finishing post.
I cannot run away from myself.

—Franz Kafka

On a sunny and cool late September afternoon, Rick and
Ronan and I took a walk along the familiar arroyo path:
past a woman weeding near the chain-link fence that separates
the narrow neighborhood paths from the paved public path;
past two mutts that, briefly separated from their owners,
bounced along behind us for a few minutes, panting hopefully
for treats we might have stashed in our pockets. We walked
toward purplish-blue mountains; the sun was a bright bead behind us. A snapshot of another sleepy Sunday with our son. A
new week was beginning, with appointments to keep and
classes to teach and workouts to muscle through and chores to
complete and people to call/e-mail/Skype. Part of my Sunday

ritual has always been imagining how the week will roll out, eventually easing out and slowing down into the weekend, with its lightweight to-dos, writing and resting and reading hours and phone chats, all plotted and mapped around Ronan's nap times and feedings and physical therapy sessions. So began the tidy little story of a week. Or so it would seem to an outsider.

The seasons were changing; time was passing. A few hours earlier Rick had stood on a ladder in Ronan's walk-in closet for almost an hour, filling shelves and hangers with outdoor gear and new sweaters and socks and shoes. Clothes for a bigger baby, a little boy. I watched him for a while, Ronan on my shoulder, and then the two of us retreated to the living room couch, where I tried to make a to-do list and found that I could not. I could no longer flip ahead to 2012 in my calendar. I didn't dare look at the following week of 2011. This small thing, whisking ahead in my old-fashioned paper planner, something I once loved to do—look at all those activities coming up! Check out the sparkly, challenging future!—filled me with dread, with haunting, unanswerable questions. *When will Ronan die? October 2012? July? Two months from now? Tomorrow? During which week and which year? Next year or the next?* Planners, I decided, are about planning to be immortal, and we all assume that we'll get another day, another week, another year. It's part of how we pretend we won't die. But when you have lived with and cared for and loved a child who is actively dying (or at least dying more quickly than the rest of us are), you learn to live in the present moment.

It was an uncomfortable, difficult lesson, one I had been given the opportunity to absorb more fully at the "Being with Dying" training session at the Upaya Zen Center in Santa Fe a few weeks earlier. The four-day retreat of meditation, teachings, and work practice was designed for hospice care workers and others who are actively caring for dying people and wish to integrate a contemplative meditation practice with compassionate end-of-life care. The idea is that a person who is hysterical is not the best companion for someone who is experiencing the final moments of life. The weekend was designed to help care workers cultivate a loving presence for their patients or loved ones. I signed us up because soon after Ronan's diagnosis I realized that Buddhism might be the only religious or philosophical system that has any true integrity around death, which is often treated as an issue to be avoided instead of an inevitable reality.

The first meal at Upaya—a beautifully tended community of temples, adobe structures, and vegetable and flower gardens—was the only one when we would not be observing "noble silence." When I was asked why Rick and I were at the retreat, I said, just this once, that our baby was terminally ill. The woman I told, who I'd later discover was a student in the Buddhist chaplaincy program, nodded her head. She did not react with histrionics or howls or a grimace or apologies. Feeling a palpable sense of relief, I realized again that the effort of dealing with Ronan's illness was divided between my own emotional maintenance and the management of other people's reac-

tions, assumptions, accusations, or bland offerings of comfort/
Bible verses/platitudes/pity. Here I had tossed death across the
table at a stranger who looked straight at it without blinking.
There's something to this Zen business, I thought, and finished up my
vegetarian rice and beans that had been prepared (we were told)
by Jane Fonda's personal chef, a woman with red-orange hair
and soft-looking hands. For the next few days, as a member of
the lunch cleanup crew, I scrubbed big wooden boats of salad
and beans and rice. I secured leftover squares of cornbread in
plastic bags labeled with the date. The residents moved quietly
from building to building, their hands folded inside front
pouches. There were edible flowers in our food. Between sessions everyone quietly drank cups of mint tea.

Having integrity is different from having answers. If anything, Buddhism offers very little in the way of consolation,
acknowledging that nobody really knows what happens to us
as we are dying (during the "labor" of dying, as our teachers
put it) or after we die. "I don't console," Roshi Joan, one of the
retreat leaders, told us in one of the first sessions, and I was
strangely relieved. What could possibly console me? What
event or success or accomplishment or experience could ever be
compensatory for the loss of a child? No, it wasn't consolation
I needed or desired, but the tools to walk through this fire
without being consumed by it.

Too bad one was left to contemplate this while attempting
to meditate, to "not think," an activity I have always found
maddening if not impossible. But meditate we did at Upaya—

for up to three hours a day, beginning at seven o'clock in the morning. After the second hour of meditation on the second day, after hours of working in the kitchen in silence, eating in silence, walking in silence and finding none of it "noble," I felt as though I were moving inside a dark and dangerously heavy circle of sadness. A gong was ringing in my chest. I'd felt it before, on the day of Ronan's diagnosis, when I had also felt intimately connected to all of the people I knew or had known who had lost someone they deeply loved. I broke the noble silence around two o'clock in the afternoon with hysterical sobs after motioning Rick out of the quiet library and into our car, parked in the lot. "I can't do this," I said. "It's too much. I just want to be with Ronan." The not-thinking of meditation left me with only this ringing, a sonar sound that grew and grew, attracting more grief. I could not even begin to approach it. It was like walking into a screaming mouth. Rick convinced me to stay, at least through the next session. Through tears, I agreed.

The next session began with photographs of dying people or the "death portraits" of people who had just died. Death, in the Christian tradition, is linked with life only in the sense that the sacrifice of Jesus cancels out the tragedy of death, overcomes death for the one who has been granted eternal life on account of his or her faith in this very possibility. It is the ultimate overcomer narrative, the "light in the darkness."

In the Buddhist tradition, dying is an inevitable part of life. Learning how to live is about learning how to die, both figuratively and literally. Dying to delusions. Dying to the relentless and unending demands of the ego. We were reminded that everyone we know or love or will know or love or have known or loved will someday die (I thought of the lyrics of the Flaming Lips song "Do You Realize"); that our physical bodies, our intelligence, our wealth, our careers and our relationships—our whole identity—will be of no use to us in that final moment. All must come unbound and undone. All will unravel. It's one thing to accept this on an intellectual level, but it was an entirely different experience to hear those truths spoken aloud while looking at the faces of people who had just died, some of them showing the marks of struggle, others peaceful, some newly born, others so thin the bones of the face looked almost transparent. Some with open eyes, fearful eyes, open mouths, clenched fists, soft baby skulls. I had the thought that this was perhaps my first moment of being an adult, and that I was, just now, finally prepared to be a mother to Ronan. Other people had weathered this, I thought. So could I.

But I began to feel a drop in my stomach whenever I saw a new baby out in the world—in part because the mother who looked at her baby as if he would outlive her had disappeared for me, that blissful, sleepless and wacky time, but also because I was now uncomfortably aware of the fact that all of those babies will die somehow, someday, and maybe sooner than we liked to think or imagine, leaving behind a grief-stricken path of mourners. Everyone seemed to be walking around with the shadow of a skeleton following close behind. Everyone felt impermanent and in danger. In a sense, that's true, and people working in hospice are intimately aware of this.

Hospice workers often create rituals in the months and weeks and days and hours before a person dies. They might haul out photographs and arrange them on the bed, make videos of the ocean or another favorite place, encourage reunions with estranged family members, offer the choice of reconciliation through letters, phone calls, invitations. One woman dying of a progressive, incurable illness decided to stop eating and have a "living wake." For weeks people came to tell her the stories of her life—how they would remember her, why they loved her. Others create altars, write songs, throw parties. It's a way of honoring life without privileging that individual life above any other, which doesn't make it any less special. Do we become what happens to us? In Christianity, yes. We're saved. In Buddhism, no. You are bigger than yourself, elemental and amazing and true, but you are also not so important, not so terribly special. You are as impermanent and transient as any other being on this earth at any other time in history. No heavenly reunions, no special ribbons or crowns, just passage into what we do not know.

On that fall Sunday several weeks after the training, I was browsing the news online when I stumbled upon a link: *Dr. Oz recommends one-minute ways to live a little longer.* Last year I would have read each suggestion and maybe tried to do one or two of them, maybe all of them, hoping to thicken that planner a bit, add a few more months and years, without realizing that's what I was doing. Nine months into Ronan's diagnosis, sitting with his little boy body snuggled securely in my lap, smelling his garlicky hummus breath and trying to loosen sleepers from his long eyelashes, all I could think was—why not just live?

I was motivated to unearth the book *Zen Action, Zen Person*, which I had studied for a comparative religion class at Harvard years ago. The pages are thick with yellow highlighter and my illegible margin notes. I vividly remember finishing the last page at Widener Library on a cold fall day, and later that night, blurry with fatigue, talking with a friend several times on the phone, changing the thesis for my term paper after every conversation. We had been charged with using Buddhist philosophy to make "moral sense" of a particular event that occurred during the Holocaust, an incident of ordinary men acting in an extraordinarily evil way. Buddhism felt slippery to me, too inclusive, floppy. I felt as if I had emptied my head in the cavernous Widener stacks. Nothing had stuck to my brain. Images of Jesus and Mary kept floating through my vision, which didn't help. But Buddhism seemed to have little to cling to, and it seemed to lack the condemnation that I felt the situation deserved and that I kept trying to sneak into my paper. There was no cage to put around what had happened; no code to decipher the meaning, moral or otherwise.

Thirteen years later I flipped through the book and thought, *Zen action, Zen baby. This is Ronan.* Up to that point, although I had acknowledged what Ronan was teaching me about being a human being with this myth of his life, I had actively resisted thinking of him as a teacher, some kind of baby guru, because I'd felt that it somehow justified his suffering, or made the gravity of the loss somehow less aching, less real, less intense. As I reacquainted myself with the book, Ronan's way of being in the world did begin to make him seem like a baby sage; he fit perfectly the nickname his cousin Iain had given him—Baby Buddha.

I am not a Buddhist, or at least not a very good one, although arguably a Buddhist would try to go beyond rigid judgments of good or bad. No parsing, no taking this and not that thought or feeling, only deep acceptance, mindful awareness. Easier said, written or thought than done. I desire, defend and distract on a daily basis. Meditation makes me want to scream, even though I feel its calming benefits hours later. I am full of the poisons of envy, anger, greed, all of it, and much of the time I do not examine the root of these emotions or their effects on others or the world. Which makes me human, I guess, and flawed, and in this flaw is the seed of perfection and peace. Or at least that's what I gathered at Upaya.

I decided that I could plan for tomorrow, at least tentatively, and one of the weekly appointments on the calendar was Ronan's meeting with our physical therapist. I glanced over her notes from the previous week:

Ronan stood three times at the table. Helped his hands and feet elongate with assisted play with plastic farm

animals. Also worked on his mouth with a gloved hand
to help practice swallowing and closed mouth breathing
with more active lip movements. He enjoyed helping
hold my gloved hand and it was clear when he was done.

We kept these narratives, written on yellow pieces of paper,
in a folder—worried, I think, that we'd forget what Ronan did
from moment to moment. A collection of little "he did" lists.
Not a ritual for dying, but little rituals of living, moments
from Ronan's life. I thought about what Frank, another of our
teachers at Upaya, said to Rick and me on the last day when we
told him about Ronan and thanked him for his presence, his
stories, his wisdom: "Remember that there's a whole person
behind whatever physical affect presents itself." Writing about
him was a way to remember Ronan and to honor all the moments of his short life.

During our break on the final day of the retreat at Upaya, I
walked up the road and found a series of trails—perfect for a
trail run or a meander or just a brisk walk in the morning. The
echo of hammers and the sound of Spanish floated over the
empty path. I did feel a lift of sadness, a weight removed, or if
not removed, then acknowledged. This was the path I would
walk. I didn't have to "like" it or even "manage" it, but I did
have to accept it. As the other dragon moms reminded me in
the weeks after Ronan's diagnosis, I had no other choice. This
is part of being an adult, I thought, part of being a parent. I
thought about something Roshi Joan had said the day before:

"You feed and wash the baby, even if you know it will die in the morning." She hadn't been speaking directly to me, of course, she'd been telling a story, but she might as well have whispered in my ear—the words went straight in, and this time they stuck.

Back at Upaya, I walked down to the small shrine on one of the tree-lined paths that twist and wind behind the buildings. Under a large tree are offerings made by visitors, residents, teachers: a Buddha statue holding flowers, a corner of fabric, a rock that reads "baby girl," a bottle of Coke swinging on a string from a branch, pieces of glass arranged in a circle in the dirt and flashing in the sun. Things placed by living people. In the distance a deer bolted through trees to the road. A sky striped with the beginnings of sunset. The windmill was still in the early evening.

No matter how old Ronan may have lived to be, his body would have failed him, he would have died. It's a common thing, when someone has a life-limiting illness, to say that the body is "failing" him or her. But according to this understanding the only way our bodies wouldn't fail us would be if they remained immortal, if they never got old, or diseased. If they never changed. If we were gods. If we, quite simply, didn't die. It is a unique and terrible privilege to witness the entire arc of a life, to see it through from its inception to its end. But it is also an opportunity to love without a net, without the future, without the past, but right now. I didn't want to be a hysterical mess during Ronan's final moments; I wanted to be loving and calm. I wanted to be a witness. I wanted to sharpen what was essential in my life and let some of the endlessly worrying externalities go fuzzy. I wanted a less bossy brain, a less insistent heart, less clutch at the life of my baby.

Buddhism instructs its followers to be at ease, always, with not knowing, with uncertainty. I realized over the first nine months of Ronan's diagnosis—from January to September—that I didn't know a single thing: not my own mind, not my own heart, not what drives me or inhibits me or makes me who I am. Everything, truly, was and is uncertain. Does it take a true skeptic to be a true believer? Maybe.

But what about the unbinding that the Buddhists talk about, those last moments before the final moment of life? If hospice care workers and family members tried to create the story of a person's journey, working with their memories and victories and losses, putting together this unique puzzle through picture and narrative, Ronan's story was like a puzzle with no pieces. What did he have to lose? A baby with no memory, the senses dimming and then entirely dark, that mysterious and magical organ of the brain just running out of steam, out of juice, out of *prana* or spirit or whatever. The winner of this prize or this medal or the mother of this many or the resident of this town or the teacher of this institution or the member of this family or the partner of this person or the singer of this song or the writer of this book or the creator of this theory or the spokesperson for that product or the person who was friends with that famous person who was famous at that time or the person of this list or the thinker of this thought or the person of this type, race, color, body, category, background, class held no meaning. For Ronan, it never did. There was us, and him, and that was it. Frank told us, "Remember that to him, you are the two faces of God." All he had to lose, in that scenario, was Rick and me. We could not follow him where he was going; he would no longer need us.

But Ronan still needed me on that Sunday afternoon in September, and I took him out for another walk. I felt the weight of his head against my chest, the vibrations of his coos and snorts and his one word, "gee." I had a great view of his toothy smile. I held his toes and combed the ducktail of curls at the back of his head with my fingers. I was literally attached to him. "Wear your baby!"—all the "natural" mothering books suggested when I read them while I was pregnant, and wear Ronan I did, my most precious accessory.

At Upaya our teachers told us that to be fully present for a person who is dying you must have a strong back and a soft front. Most of us, they pointed out, live with the reverse. We are outwardly defensive, and because we resist compassion we are actually weaker. A broken heart is an open heart, and there exists great strength in a shaky vulnerability. Ronan was the ultimate soft front. The most dear, the most heartbreaking physical representation of anything I had ever in my life been able to give, been given, or cared about. And all of it, someday, like Ronan, would be lost.

On this sleepy Sunday, the sky ink-blue and darkening, Ronan's eyes drooping, I wondered if it was little more than semantics or brain gymnastics. I knew that after Ronan was gone, I would listen for him each night, and his face would be the first face I'd think of in the morning, the face I'd always miss. This missing would be a daily ritual for the rest of my life. And I would continue scribbling, hoping it would help me reach the end intact or sane, and I did it knowing that any scribble might be my last. I will look at the many photos of him, wanting to remember, wanting to forget, longing to reexperience particular moments or recall little details about his face. And the world was still the world, and yet . . .

One of our teachers at Upaya told us that Jizo Bodhisattva, the boatman who ferries the dead across the river, the companion of travelers between worlds, is also the guardian of children. Was it too much to ask to be on that same boat, if even for a moment, ferried across with my son in my arms, or worn in a front pack? I'd sit at the back and let his feet dangle in the water, slip the smallest coin in his mouth, another in mine, pay for the passage of both of us. Because I know, in whatever final lucid moment I have before I die, I will see Ronan's face, and I will wish I could hold him one last time before I, too, am released from this body and make my own crossing from this life into whatever comes next.

23

There was a story I often told myself when I thought about "after Ronan." It wasn't a place I wanted to visit, but the story helped me go there, and I hoped it would help me visit him, or the dream feeling of him, until I was old and had forgotten everything else. Part memory, part dream, part wishful thinking.

The afterlife story is this: I'm on Inishmore, an island off the West Coast of Ireland, walking toward Dun Aengus, an ancient fort that has been eroding for centuries; half of it has already fallen into the ocean below. I visited the Aran Islands with friends in 1995, but in the dream memory I am alone. I scale rocky famine walls that crisscross the landscape, passing cottages and a few isolated people. A fog descends. I can no longer see my hands or where my footsteps are taking me, so I turn around and walk in the other direction, away from the sound of the water. I am curious and unafraid. My mouth tastes of seawater and wet wool. My feet and legs hurt, but not in an unpleasant way. In fact, I feel sporty and alive. My blood is warm and I can hear my heartbeat, steady and fast but not frantic. The color of the sky begins to change; there is sun behind the thick reach of gray-white clouds. Slowly, it gets warmer and warmer. There are more people on the road now, nodding at me as they pass. The sleepy town is no longer sleeping. I walk down the dirt road, past a yard where baby clothes are fluttering on a clothesline, still too wet and heavy to flap in the wind, which is gentle and sea fragrant. The sun is strong now, almost tropical strength. I reach the shore of a small rocky beach littered with seaweed, sit down, then lie down and finally fall asleep. I wake up to barking, splashing and my face pounding with sunburn. Sound echoes and astounds here as it does when you rise from a dream state; it refracts and shifts like light, like moods.

I look out over the water and see them on a jagged outcropping of rock: a few dark seals, their sleek and impossible bodies—so graceful, so smooth—slipping in and out of the water. They move from rock to sea and back again, shaking their delicately whiskered faces, water glittering like suntouched glass from their whiskers, tails powerful and flapping. Ronan: in Irish, little seal. Ronin: in Hebrew, song. I watch them for a long time, those seals, dipping in and out of the water, cool and calm and singing.

AFTERWORD

Much has happened since the completion of this book.

Ronan died peacefully at home in the early morning hours of February 15, 2013. During the last six months of his life, the realities of Tay-Sachs disease made the act of daily living difficult for him, and finally, impossible. His hospice nurse was on call at all hours of the night and day during those final weeks and days, and I am so grateful to Mariposa Pediatric Hospice and especially to Cynthia Baber for her kindness and compassion, for her in-the-moment guidance of how to make Ronan comfortable, for her help in making his dying process one marked by dignity and painless passage. Ronan was a boy who was loved every second of his life, and my gratitude extends not just to his caretakers, but to all the people—friends, family, strangers, colleagues—who allowed him into their life, either in person or through the reading of this book. Although Ronan was afflicted by the most hideous of illnesses, we should all have such an end: surrounded by people who love us, and who will hold us until we take our last breath, wrap us in a shroud, watch over us, and then mourn us for the rest of their lives.

Rick and I separated not long after this book was finished, and we eventually divorced. The amount of stress placed on a couple losing their child to a slow and degenerative disease cannot be underestimated. It is like falling asleep every night in the mouth of the world, not sure when and if you'll be swallowed, and how. To be in this constant state of hypervigilance and anticipatory grief revealed the cracks in our relationship, and also revealed the very human capacity for destruction and cruelty. Nobody grieves in the same way, and in that manic and churning moment, it is very difficult to understand another person's process and often, to forgive it. That Rick and I failed to assist each other through the death of our child is a reflection of our relationship and our personal flaws, not of our mutual, unquantifiable love for Ronan.

In much of this book I rail frequently against the concept of luck, which I do believe is a spurious—if highly seductive—notion. I have thought often about this in the months following Ronan's death, a strange, shifting time that is marked by the feeling of release that he is no longer suffering and the unavoidable feeling of rock bottom sadness that I will never see him again. And, of course, the strange but very real guilt that I am still here and he is not. I cannot say that I've revised my views on the matter of luck, not completely, but I can say that I feel lucky to have been Ronan's mother, and to have been a witness at both his birth and at his death, the second being, of course, terrible, but also deeply profound. We like to romanticize life. We're intent on extending it, living it long and hard and purposefully, whatever that might mean to us, but the reality is that sometimes it's better to be dead than to live on in a compromised body with no hope of recovery. And when we die it is better not to do so alone.

People often referred to Ronan as "Zen baby," or "the Buddha boy." He did have this energetic presence: non-judgmental, soft and immobile, without panic or ego or desire. Effortless, perfect beauty. In this way, he was purely innocent in the way that those of us with normal cognitive function and more normally operating bodies could never be. He did not know he was dying, although everyone around him was inevitably acutely focused on that fact. Because Ronan put other people in touch with their own mortality, without any effort on his part he encouraged a very ego-driven activity in others: bravery. But this was a bravery not focused on bravado, with which it is often mistaken. It was unconcerned with any desired outcome of recognition or fame or fortune; instead, it was about living honestly, with all the veils pulled off your eyes, with the flaws and beauties of the world open and alive to your imagination. He forced me and many others to live our truest lives, which inevitably meant making some difficult decisions.

There's a line from my favorite Louise Gluck poem, "The Wild Iris," which states "at the end of my suffering there was a door." This end is literal death for all of us, at some point, as it was for Ronan, yet small but extraordinary moments of re-demption happen in ordinary lives all the time. Something ir-replaceable is taken from you; something irreplaceable is given to you. This one gift is not equal to the other, it is not a trade, or a salve, or a fix, but it is what life presents, what it offers, and sometimes what it demands, even if, and especially when, you feel you don't deserve it.

In the last six months of Ronan's life I fell in love with a man who took on—without judgment or hesitation—the com-plications of loving a grief-stricken, almost-divorced woman caring for her dying baby. Early on in our relationship, and many times as Ronan's condition worsened, Kent promised to be with me every step of the way. Others had made such prom-ises to me, and I had discovered how rare it is that they are kept. He kept his. He gave me hope and laughter and true con-nection and the chance for a new beginning in a time when all four seemed odd if not impossible. And because grief does not end with the loss of a person, but changes and shifts and moves in unexpected ways, he's still keeping those promises. I waited my whole life for this man, and that I met him in the midst of the most gutting loss I've ever experienced seemed, at the time, and still seems, like some mysterious, glittering gift.

This book, all the essays, I've written about Ronan amount to so many words. Sometimes, writing this book, I thought it would act as some weird, magical spell that might, against all logic or belief, save my child. But words don't save; sometimes they can barely describe. In some ways, writing this now, looking out at the mesa where Kent and I buried a lock of Ronan's snipped hair, thinking about the Rio Grande River where we scattered his hair from a hot air balloon, later thinking that some strands might be used by a bird to build a nest, or just become a part of the deep ground, I think how strange it is to try and create on a two-dimensional page a flesh and blood person, or to convey the singular meaning of a singular life. But that is what we want to do when we love someone completely: we want everyone to understand our incomprehensible, stumbling hearts. We want the wonder to be made clear to anyone who might listen to what we say, for people to fathom what feels unfathomable, to experience all the dreamscapes where our beloveds live on.

The night Ronan died my friend Jenny had a dream about him. In this dream he was standing on the edge of an ocean, next to a boat. The sun was shining, the waves were crashing against the cliffs behind him. Her description reminded me of Greece: pale sands, color-rich water, bright, unexpected angles of light. A regal setting. He was dressed in some kind of royal armor, and his hair flew long and blond from his helmet. He was saying something to her, but she couldn't hear him over the roar of the ocean, the rush of the wind. But he was beautiful and strong, she said, and proud. He was headed for adventure, for life on some other shore and he was ready—he was prepared—to go. I also have not altered my views on the afterlife, but it is to this grown boy, this young man, glimpsed in a parallel dream universe, that I address this final note:

Ronan, thank you. Thank you for choosing me as your mother, for every inch of your beautiful body I made with mine, for your sweet and uncomplicated presence. I wanted to save you. What a terrible irony that you were, in the end, the one who saved me. *Slainte, little man.* You are remembered, you precious, irreplaceable boy, and you are missed.

ACKNOWLEDGMENTS

A book like this—and any book, really—is never written in a vacuum or without help. Writers write alone, but we are also of the world, and I am deeply grateful to and humbled by the one of which I am fortunate enough to be a part. Writing this book often felt like running an endless race, a lonely and troubling one, although I was never alone. It is not an exaggeration to say that the people (often strangers) who accompanied me—cheering, weeping, encouraging, reading, listening, talking or just silently witnessing—have made it possible for me to live through the experience of losing my child and tell his story. This—my planet of friends—is an ecosystem that has quite literally sustained me. All of you, too many to name here, have allowed me to spin in your generous orbit and, in so many different ways, have grounded me. You know who you are, and from the truest and wildest part of my heart, I thank you.

There are several people I'd like to name specifically: Jennifer Weber, for her early suggestion to write about Ronan and her behind-the-scenes brilliance; Lisa Glatt, Bernadette

Murphy, Dani Shapiro, Sarah Sentilles, Gina Frangello and Rachel Dewoskin, for the intelligence and insights they brought to early drafts and sections of this book as well as for their loving and loyal friendship. Thank you to Tara Ison, Julia Goldberg, Carrie Scanga, Elizabeth Tannen, Annik Lafarge, Jennifer Pastiloff, Catherine Davis and Emily Miles, for loving me enough to read and listen and cry and rage, sometimes endlessly and at all hours, day or night. Thank you to my parents, Roger and Mary Rapp, who love and support me even when I mystify them and to whom I can always tell the truth. Thank you to Rob Roberge, Chris Abani, Robert Wilder, Kate Weldon Le-Blanc, Jenny George, Eloise Klein Healy, Kaliq Simms, Amy Dixon, Caeli Bourbeau, Alissa Tschetter-Siedschlaw, Cheryl Strayed, Colin Moore, Steve Hirst, Barbara Pitkin, Edmund Santurri, Andrew Primm, Nouf al-Qasimi, Monika Bustamante, Amy Silverman, Chris Simpson, Ryann Watson, Megan Reif, Terri Rolland, Emma Simmons, Wendy Ortiz, Sandy Lee, Carin van Olst, Juliana Jones, Donna and Lew Bagby, and Gareth Batterbee for crucial reminders about hope and possibility in a time when there appeared to be none. Thank you to Nancy Conyers and Libby Costin for rooms full of light and beauty in which to write and think and be.

Thank you to my friends and colleagues Matt Donovan and Dana Levin and to all the faculty and staff at the Santa Fe University of Art and Design for the time and space to work on this project; thank you to Tod Goldberg and the faculty and staff at the University of California-Riverside Palm Desert MFA program for giving me a writerly home. Thank you to my students for teaching me. Thank you to the Fundación Valparaiso in Mojacar, Spain, for much-needed solitude and writing space. Thank you to the Upaya Zen Center for facilitating the crucial work of integrating contemplative practice into end-of-life care. Thank you to the editors of *The New York Times, The Rumpus, The Santa Fe Reporter, The Nervous Breakdown, Slate, The Huffington Post, Bark* and *Salon* for telling parts of Ronan's story.

Thank you to Ronan's doctors and therapists, especially Janet Padma Mandell, Ashleigh Linkenheimer, Alana and Dawn, for giving him comfort and for accepting him just the way he was, at every stage of his life.

Thank you to the National Tay-Sachs and Allied Diseases Association for everything they do for affected families and children, and a special roaring thank-you to the dragon mothers and fathers who taught me how to be a parent. Thank you, Becky Benson, for bringing me so many times from darkness into light.

A hallelujah-style, double high five thank-you to my agent, the fierce and funny Dorian Karchmar, who believed in this book from the very beginning and who is my advocate and my friend. Thank you to my fabulous editor, Andrea Walker, for her incredible mind, brilliant editorial insight and sparkling kindness to a writer working her way out of the dark. A heartfelt bow to everyone at the Penguin Press for making this book happen, and in just this way.

And finally, thank you to Rick Louis, who loved Ronan the way all fathers should love their sons: without condition and without strings and with the force of his whole heart. This book is for our boy, but it is also for you.

SUGGESTED READINGS

Armstrong, Karen, *A Short History of Myth*

Atwood, Margaret, *Alias Grace*

Bashō, *The Complete Haiku*

Bishop, Elizabeth, *The Complete Poems, 1927–1979*

Brooks, Geraldine, *Year of Wonders: A Novel of the Plague*

Case, Neko, and Her Boyfriends, *Furnace Room Lullaby* (album)

Dalley, Stephanie, *Myths from Mesopotamia: Creation, the Flood, Gilgamesh, and Others*

Ford, Katie, *Deposition: Poems*

Gluck, Louise, *The Wild Iris*

Halifax, Joan, *Being with Dying: Cultivating Compassion and Fearlessness in the Presence of Death*

Havel, Václav, *Open Letters: Selected Writings, 1965–1990*

Heaney, Seamus, *Opened Ground, Poems, 1966–1996*

Kafka, Franz, *Letters to Milena*

Kantonen, T. A., *Life After Death*

Kasulis, T. P., *Zen Action: Zen Person*

Kenyon, Jane, *Otherwise: New and Selected Poems*

Kushner, Harold, *When Bad Things Happen to Good People*

Levin, Dana, *Sky Burial*

Lewis, C. S., *A Grief Observed*

Mann, Thomas, *The Magic Mountain*

McCullers, Carson, *The Member of the Wedding*

Neruda, Pablo, *100 Love Sonnets*

Pardi, Philip, *Meditations on Rising and Falling*

Plath, Sylvia, *The Collected Poems*

Robinson, Marilynne, *Gilead: A Novel*

Shelley, Mary, *Frankenstein*

Sherwood, Frances, *Vindication: A Novel*

Szymborska, Wislawa, *Poems: New and Collected*

Weil, Simone, *Waiting for God*

PERMISSIONS